ESCAPING A
NARCISSISTIC
MARRIAGE

Published in Australia by
TRU Media
PO Box 256, Doreen, VIC 3754, Australia

First published in Australia 2024
Copyright © Suzanna James 2024

All rights reserved. No part of this publication may be reproduced, stored in a retrieval system, or transmitted, in any form or by any means without the prior written permission of the publisher, nor be otherwise circulated in any form of binding or cover other than that in which it is published and without a similar condition being imposed on the subsequent purchaser.

National Library of Australia Cataloguing in Publication entry

 A catalogue record for this book is available from the National Library of Australia

Title: *Escaping a Narcissistic Marriage*
Previously published as *Divorce and the Aftermath*

ISBN: 978-0-6486225-0-5 (paperback)
ISBN: 978-0-6486225-1-2 (epub)

Cover design by Wizdiz, 99designs
Layout and typesetting by Sophie White Design

Printed by Ingram Spark

This book is memoir. It reflects the author's present recollections of experiences over time. Some names and characteristics have been changed, some events have been compressed, and some dialogue has been recreated.

Escaping a Narcissistic Marriage

A MEMOIR OF BETRAYAL

SUZANNA JAMES

DEDICATION

To my mother, Elsie, who has always been a tower of strength and has taught me to believe in myself. A woman who has gone through her own battles in life and taught me that no matter what life throws at you to never give up; she is not just my mother; she was and is my best friend.

Also to my dear friend, Andrea, who has been my best friend for the last 28 years. She lived in Brisbane and even though she was so far away, there was not a day went by that she did not phone me. She was so supportive over so many awful years.

More importantly, she never judged me over the many mistakes that I may have made and I believe that to be true friendship.

AUTHOR'S NOTE

How many times do we ignore our instincts and what our investigative mind is trying to tell us? Well, eventually we have no choice but to listen. That is what my story is about.

After 19 years of marriage, it suddenly dawned on me that it was time to face the ugly truth. So, I did... after it was staring at me fair square in my face. There was no denying the truth any longer, not as I had done for so many years prior.

Escaping a Narcissistic Marriage is dedicated to all the men and women in the world who gave of themselves selflessly to their marital relationship, only to end up with feelings of betrayal and stripped of all their self-esteem. Those whose families have been torn apart purely for lust.

My book expresses a way of regaining one's self-pride, turning the pain around, and showing how making life-changing decisions whilst going through such emotional turmoil, can only make it so much worse.

In telling my story and the mistakes I may have made in the hope it somehow helps those of you in a similar situation understand your journey.

The positive outcomes that you—and *only* you—can bring into your life, no matter what happens to you, can be the turning point at any given time. It can be a life-changing experience, allowing yourself to move forward for the better.

I call it a better life. After all, you must remember it's not what happens to you, it's how you deal with it.

I hope you can deal with it better than I did.

Chapter 1

MY STORY

My story begins 22 years ago, when I chose not to listen to my instincts and started dating my now ex-husband Bryce.

The telltale signs were there all those years ago but it took me over two decades to wake up. After all, some people never do.

Bryce was eight years my junior, arrogant and with loads of confidence. He held a certain charm when I first met him. Bryce liked everyone to think he was extremely successful and had plenty of money to play with but that was not reality... in the beginning anyway.

He was—and is to this day—a compulsive liar.

I fell in love with him even though I knew he was very controlling. Unfortunately, I mistook that for believing him to be a 'real man', a tower of strength. How wrong I was! He was the type of person who would help anyone in a crisis, particularly married women who were going through relationship problems. As time went by, I learned he just liked to play the hero. It was all for self-gratification, not for the right reasons.

My first clue was the pornographic books he continually

hid in either the boot of his car or a locked briefcase. You know, the type of pornography that comes in a sealed plastic bag. Even after being caught red-handed, he denied ownership; his excuses were imaginative but believable.

I should have realised who he really was then but I didn't. Bryce was a romantic, and I was in love with the thought of being in love. My mother, who constantly reminded me that love is blind, was so right. I should have listened to her.

Bryce and I dated for a couple of years before we married, and I have to say that even now, it seems like yesterday. When I look back, I cannot understand why I did not recognise what was always in front of me. Bryce was the best liar I had ever met. When we first started dating, I used to find love letters in his car. He would tell me they were a joke from one of his friends, and I believed him. It should have been another clue, another red-flag. Where was my intelligence?

Our wedding day finally arrived, with no expense spared, but something just was not right. I felt incredibly ill and doubled-over in pain. So much so that I could barely walk down the aisle. Later, I came to understand that my body was trying to tell me this was a big mistake; one I would regret for the rest of my life. This is called listening to your instincts!

After being married for a couple of years, Bryce asked

if I would have his children. I was 35 years old at the time and already had two teenage children from a previous marriage yet those three little words always got to me: "I love you," he would say, and probably too often.

It's funny when I think back to those early days and realise the universe had given me so many clues as to whom Bryce really was, but I always ignored them. Even after being married for less than 12 months, I had found a private bank account where he had saved all his commission cheques, leading me to think he was doing poorly in his job and therefore money was tight. The arguments would follow but he always managed to give me hope, and we would move on as we always did. This habit would take me years to break.

Not long after that, I became pregnant. When the time came for me to give birth to our first son, I was 35. Our second child arrived when I was 37. Bryce was over the moon, a real doting dad. He was wonderful for the first couple of years of fatherhood and that was probably the happiest time in our married life but it would not last long.

Not long after giving birth to Bryce's second son, everything started to change. Life was never to be the same. Not for me. Not for our children.

Bryce started coming home from work very late at night, always with many excuses. One of my favourites was that he was with a client. I always believed him.

As I said before, there were plenty of clues the universe would send me, and so many occasions but looking back, I don't think I wanted to know.

When our second son was about six months of age, we decided to sell and move to a new area. It was just what we needed – a new start. In time, I learned it truly doesn't matter how many times you move, you always take the problem with you.

We sold our first home after renovating, then moved into our new home. I thought we were a happy family, but I was so very wrong.

It wasn't long after we moved that Bryce started to go on interstate trips with his work, and the tale started to unfold. A tale that would nearly destroy everything I ever believed in.

Bryce returned home from work early one afternoon only to tell me that he was leaving. I was devastated. Our youngest child was about to turn one, and his father was not going to be around.

I continually asked myself, "How can this doting father, my husband, turn into this monster that I don't know?"

There was no other way to describe him.

He did not offer any explanation at the time except that he had been seeing a psychiatrist; she had told him that he had been persecuted by me.

How dramatic.

I knew then he was lying; he had not been seeing a

psychiatrist at all. Bryce was just manipulating me to make me feel bad.

I will never forget the word 'persecuted'. What was he talking about? Up to that point, I thought our lives were not that bad. What did he see that I didn't? I continued to question myself, which is what he wanted; to place the blame on myself when he had a plan all along. It is called manipulation, and Bryce was—and is still—a master at it.

Bryce's family—mother, father, brothers and girlfriends—had just been down the previous weekend, all making the trek from the country for a dinner party. Everyone was so happy. From memory, they were all dancing and laughing. So, how could one day make a difference? It had to be a bad dream. How could this be? I continued to question myself day and night.

I don't think I will ever forget that feeling when Bryce packed his bags and got into his car one cloudy afternoon and didn't even look back. His four-year-old son chased his car down the road, screaming hysterically, "Daddy, come back!"

Our son was an emotional mess. It broke my heart and changed me and my little four-year-old's life forever, leaving my child with insecurities he would feel for the rest of his life. I will always remember that date; it was my dad's birthday – February 18th, 1992. We had been getting ready to go to his birthday party.

We went through so much pain. I lost weight rapidly

through shock, and the days grew longer and longer. The nights were worse. I drank to rid myself of the pain, took up smoking, and cried each day and every night. I had no idea where Bryce had gone; he was missing for a month and then eventually he made contact. He wasn't even with us for Easter. I continually asked myself how he could just disappear, leaving me and our boys in so much pain.

He told me it was over, he hated me, and I couldn't quite come to terms with his insults or his change of personality.

Bryce would visit infrequently, calling me a fucking slut as he walked through the front door but the words that followed, I will never forget.

He would look me straight in the eye, saying to me repeatedly that he wished I would die. This was not the same man I had married. I could not believe what I was hearing. There had to be some reason for Bryce's change of behaviour, and of course there was!

Just remember that word 'manipulation'.

Chapter 2

GOTCHA FINALLY

As the story unravelled and the truth reared its ugly head, I would understand so much more clearly. When a man or woman acts in this way, it always means guilt, that there is someone else waiting in the shadows. A change of behaviour is a sure signal; even their behaviour in bed is a giveaway.

After realising this was the way it was going to be, I decided I had to be strong and regain what self-respect I had left. I had to move on.

I didn't know what to do about anything at the time, but I knew I needed to get custody of my children, needed to protect them. I went to a lawyer who asked me where Bryce had been before all this happened. I told him he had been at a conference with his work in Sydney.

Without even blinking, he said, "Your husband is having an affair."

I told the lawyer there was no way Bryce would do that to me.

My initial thought was that he had suffered a nervous breakdown, although most of my friends and family said the same as my lawyer – Bryce was having an affair. Of course, I continued to defend him. In fact, I will never forget that dark, dismal and stormy Mother's Day in 1992 when his parents came to visit me, blaming me for upsetting Bryce. I can hear his mother now as she continually questioned me and kept asking what I had done to her son. She felt he could be suicidal, and it was entirely my fault.

When I told them that my lawyer suspected an affair, they were horrified and said, "Not our son, he would never do that."

Later I became aware of just how naive I was; my lawyer was right.

He told me that when your partner changes so drastically, you can be sure there is always someone else in the wings. I have never forgotten that, it was a moment suspended in time.

Still, I had to get on with it for the sake of my children. I had no choice. The penny dropped! I was going to be on my own and needed to provide my babies with some stability.

After being a full-time, stay-at-home mother, I knew I had to go back to work to provide a good life for them. It was all up to me. I went to night school to enable myself to get a job in real estate, and it wasn't long before I secured a position as a part-time property manager.

Bryce had even missed his youngest son's first birthday, his first steps. That was the sort of dad he had become. I know many parents would not be able to comprehend how any father or mother could miss these precious moments.

He was sharing a townhouse with an older woman about a half-hour's drive from where we were living. When I questioned who this woman was, he said she was just a friend. Once again, I believed him. Even after all that had happened, I was still oblivious. Due to the woman's age, I had no reason to suspect anything. She was 10 years older than me, and I was eight years older than Bryce. So, I never thought anything of it.

Her name was Ruth. She was 18 years his senior, and a grandmother. Why would I suspect they were having an affair? I learned later he had spent Easter with Ruth and her family in Wollongong, New South Wales.

In fact, I remember taking our boys to visit Bryce at the townhouse he was renting with Ruth. It was plush, of course; had to be for Bryce, as he had always lived in a superficial world and made out he was something he was not. I never suspected anything, but I never met Ruth either so there was no reason to be suspicious. The reason we visited was I needed to take the boys to see their dad because my eldest son would scream every day and every night. He needed Bryce, missed him terribly; I had no choice.

Every night I prayed with Bryce's grandmother's bible, prayed that he would come home. As the old saying goes,

'Be careful what you wish for'. Or, in my case, what I prayed for!

You can imagine it was the worst time in my life up to that point. This was a man who truly manipulated my life from start to finish, and I couldn't bear for my little boys to be so hurt and missing their dad so much. I just wanted my family together.

Three months had passed, and I was just getting back on my feet when lo and behold, Bryce called me on his 30th birthday to ask if he could see me. I didn't want to go but he said it was important. All this right when I was just getting my life back on track. I had even been asked out that day on a date; that was a first for me but of course, I didn't go. It was the last thing on my mind.

I met Bryce at a local hotel, and could not understand what he wanted and why he sounded so serious. Then came truth time. He blurted out that he had never meant to hurt me and that it was all a mistake. That he wanted to come home. He was so apologetic and kept telling me how much he truly loved me but insisted I must know the whole truth, the truth about Ruth – his lover, the woman he had been living with. He was covering his tracks and knew if he didn't tell me, she would. Bryce claimed he only had sex with her once. Did he think me an absolute fool? Well yes, I suppose I had given him enough reasons to think I would believe anything that came out of his mouth.

But not this time.

Later, I discovered that Bryce had spent a considerable amount of our savings to move Ruth from Wollongong to Melbourne. She was the mystery woman at the conference in Sydney that my lawyer had previously spoken of; you know, when a man changes there is always a woman involved. Ruth was the woman.

Bryce said he needed to be honest. Honest my arse. It was all manipulation. A way to get back into my life. Telling me how much he missed his family and didn't understand what had happened to him. I took the bait. After all, he was the best liar I had ever known, always sincere and believable.

It is fair to say at that time, I did not want to bring up our children by myself, it was not fair to me or to them. Little did I realise, the trust was gone forever.

I went through so much pain over the following years that could have been avoided had I realised it would be so hard to rebuild our relationship under such circumstances. If you don't have trust, you have nothing. We went to so many psychologists hoping there would be a quick fix but I learned later he couldn't even tell the truth at our weekly sessions. In fact, the psychologist later described him to me as a narcissistic personality. Who was this guy? Why did he lie so compulsively?

I let it go, and just lived my life for my children. Although, if I am to be honest, there were some happy times in those years... with the exception of the mind games Bryce would occasionally play.

We decided to move again because there were so many bad memories in our current home but this time, we decided to build our dream home.

I remember one Father's Day, we were renting a cute old cottage while our new home was being built, and life had been quite good. There was no reason to worry about anything. I was at peace with my life. However, the very day I was thinking all was great, Bryce received a text and, when I asked who it was, his reply was, "It was my boss wishing me a happy Father's Day."

My first initial thought was, *are you kidding?*

It was actually a woman named Claire. Not his boss, who I will talk about further into this story.

I thought, *please God, not again!*

My youngest son had a football game that day; it wasn't a great day, it started with an argument and ended with an argument. Bryce went one step further this time with his manipulation.

The argument was getting heated then, unexpectedly, Bryce told the boys—who were only eight and ten years old at the time—to go into the spare room with him and lock the door. He took the phone with him, removing the handle from the outside of the door so I could not get in. For the life of me, I could not understand what the hell was going on. Then I realised that I was banging on the door, making a scene whilst he was on the phone to my eldest children, telling them I was insane. Guess what? For a short time, they believed him. They could hear me yelling and banging on the door to let me in.

The boys were frightened, and God only knows what was going through their heads at the time. It wasn't until years later that I exposed him for the true bastard he was. This had become a volatile relationship; one that should not had ever been, one that was destined to finish.

However, we moved past that episode. I can't remember how, but we did. Life went back to normal for a while.

We built our dream home; it was gorgeous, a real family home. I felt this was going to be great for our kids and I finally felt that Bryce had changed. Wrong! He had just become better with his lies and deceit which, unbeknown to me, were about to further unravel.

Our family moved into our new home in December 2000. I remember thinking, *wow, what a great year for new beginnings!* I truly was the optimist.

We finally seemed happy. Then one sunny afternoon at the end of January 2001, Bryce was out in the garden speaking to a contractor about our driveway, and I was standing in our home office. As I was gazing out of the window, looking at him and thinking all was great with the world, he received a text message. By this time, I hated texts! My immediate thought was not to look, to trust him, but when you have been hurt as I had been... Curiosity got the better, I had to look.

I was shocked to see a teddy bear come up on the screen. It was from a woman named Claire asking him to call her with kisses. Remember, it was Claire some time ago who texted and wished Bryce a happy Father's Day. My stomach just cramped; *here we go again*. Our life had become a habit. There would be a few years of happiness and then Bryce would take me again and again on his merry-go-round.

As soon as Bryce came through the front door, I confronted him. He responded as he always had – with lies. "Oh, that... it was just a friend."

Yeah right.

I decided to let it go, but I couldn't get the text off my mind. My instinct was telling me there was more to this, so I planted a tape recorder behind the bookcase. It was the perfect opportunity to find out the truth about Claire; after all, her name had popped up over the last couple of years, she had to be significant.

One thing I hated was lies!

Now, I could learn the truth.

Bryce worked from home and had the house to himself whilst I was at work. I conveniently had one of those tape recorders that only activated when there was noise in the room.

That's when I started to play his game. Little did I realise, the game would consume my every thought. It became like an addiction. I had to catch him, and couldn't wait to get home and listen to the day's events.

"Hello, sweetheart," I would say when I arrived home, and then would discreetly retrieve my tape from the bookshelf and head to the shops where I would sit in my car and listen for some time.

Here I was, sitting in my car at the local supermarket, tape recorder in hand and waiting anxiously to hear the nitty gritty. However, that was not the case for some weeks as all I heard was heavy breathing, women screaming and making odd sounds. It took me a while to work out that Bryce had been looking at a porn site on his computer which, I came to learn, he did frequently during the day. So much for working!

Then, one afternoon after about a month of listening to a tape a day, I came home from work at lunchtime and took the tape recorder back with me. I was working full-time then for a large newspaper company. I will never forget sitting in the underground car park at work listening and waiting when all of a sudden, I heard voices. Sprung! I didn't know whether I was excited or heartbroken. It was Claire; she had phoned him from Surfers Paradise.

Bryce answered, and his side of the conversation went like this:

"Hello, sweetheart... Yes, I miss you too. I'm struggling here... We're trying for the kids' sake, I have to make it work this time... Yes, we'll stay in touch. I'm not going to lose you."

I still have that tape to this day. For some reason, I just could never dispose of it.

What a bastard, I thought. This was all news to me. I had no idea we were trying to hold it together. Who was this guy?

I was crushed. Once again. How many times does one have to endure her husband's infidelity? I understand what most women would be thinking right now: why would she have stuck it out so long? Allow me to explain.

Having had gone through a prior marriage and bringing up children on my own, I had a vision of giving my children the perfect family life. I didn't want to go through that again, so I hung on to that dream for as long as I could, even though it was not realistic. My children deserved to have everything I had wanted ever since I was a child – a happy home.

I had to confront him, so I did. He started with the excuses and at that point, I decided to take matters into my own hands. I knew Claire had worked with Bryce in his previous job. He travelled to Surfers Paradise on a regular basis and I remembered he had mentioned a woman named Claire he had worked with at the time, and that was where this little rendezvous started. She was also married.

My immediate thought was, *why do I have to go through this pain?* If it's good enough for me, it's good enough for her. I rang her work and enquired to her surname, pretending to be a client. Fortunately, they were listed in the local phone directory. Then, I proceeded to call her husband – a feisty Italian man who was not the type to be crossed.

I introduced myself and proceeded to fill him in on the conversation I heard between his wife and my husband. He was initially displeased but after speaking to Claire, he calmed down – she had put her own spin on it. Claire convinced her husband I was an overprotective wife, and that Bryce and she were just good friends.

He believed her, but at the same time spoke to Bryce and said if he ever found out anything different, he would fly down to Melbourne on the next plane and break his legs.

Once again, it all blew over, only to rear its ugly head with a new lover in the wings. I believe for many years later this incident, Bryce still kept in contact with Claire. Perhaps, he still does to this day.

Bryce finally landed a new job and, as I said, he was in and out of work many times over the years.

Looking back now, I believe he mixed work with pleasure, which is why he always became unstuck and always lost his job.

His excuses continued and it all became so monotonous. I wonder what was he trying to achieve? He must have been so unhappy in life. Why wasn't his family ever enough?

It really makes me wonder why men and women are

so deceitful when they could have it all. Why does anyone have to suffer, especially the children?

The next three years were not all bad, as Bryce had been working from home again. He had created his own business and was quite successful. Was even doing some cooking. Everything was starting to seem normal, just the way family life should be. Once again, I thought that maybe, finally, all I had been through had been worth hanging on for the sake of our children.

After all the heartache and endurance, my dream for my family was finally coming true. Bryce was a different person when he was not working for a company and travelling interstate all the time. The opportunities to meet other women were not possible, what with him being at home. The temptation had been removed.

Happy times were here at last, but not for long. Bryce became bored after three years working from home, and started applying for positions that took him away from us. He finally landed a National sales role. Our lives were about to change forever. None of us would ever be the same again.

Bryce had been in his new role for only a few months, and he was hardly ever home. Travelling on business regularly to all states and New Zealand frequently, something was not right again. I could feel it. My instinct was starting to kick in again.

This time, I was finally ready to move on. This time,

there was no denying the truth that I had been living a lie for years. This time, I had to face myself in the mirror.

For I had wasted 22 years of my life thinking that I could change Bryce. Let me tell you, nobody ever really changes. I learned that the hard way.

I will never forget the morning of October 16th, 2004. I was so happy. My boys were happy. Everything seemed right with the world.

It was a Saturday morning; Bryce rolled over, gave me a kiss and said, "Good morning, sweetheart."

Little did I know, my family's life was about to fall apart.

He went to have a shower and I could not turn off that little voice in my head that said I needed to check his phone. The previous day, I had been in the car with him when his phone had rung. The problem was, he did not leave it on hands-free to talk to the person on the other end. He obviously did not want me to hear the conversation and, when I asked who it was, he told me that it was just a client.

Now, I jumped out of bed whilst he was in the shower and found his phone in the car. When I took it back to bed with me, my heart was pounding. There was a message.

Did I really want to listen? There was no choice; I had to know the truth. Had he changed? No more excuses. Instinct overrode everything; I just had to listen to a message that would change our lives forever. Believe me, sometimes I wish I had never heard it.

With a deep breath, I dialled message bank 101; it was a woman named Deb saying to Bryce, 'Hi, lover, it's only me. Give me a call when you can, love you.'

I felt sick. Then I heard him returning from the bathroom, and quickly dumped the phone into my bedside table drawer. What a foolish move that was!

Bryce dressed and then went to his car only to come back in asking if I had seen his phone.

Then I really felt sick.

Before I could stop him, Bryce picked up my phone and called his. Silly me forgot to turn his phone off and, bingo! Caught red-handed.

I stumbled over my words. The phone was ringing in my drawer. I had no choice but to tell the truth. "By the way," I said. "You have a message from your lover."

He gasped. "You have to be kidding." Bryce gave me that look he always did when he was not telling the truth. There is a lot to be said about body language, his lip always went up with a slight grin.

I had come to realise that every time I saw that expression, whatever came out of his mouth was a lie.

With my heart still pounding, he had the utter gall to say it was a friend playing a joke on him. I had heard that explanation so many times before. He had obviously come to believe I was such a fool and so gullible. I was so easy to manipulate, and I suppose I had given him every reason to think that way. After all, it had taken me so many years to discover he was not real and then actually believe it.

I decided to play it cool. He even made a joke about it to our two sons, making out I was crazy, saying to them, "What a funny joke someone played on me."

Unfortunately, our boys believed him and thought I was being ridiculous. Once again, he was manipulating and getting away with it. Bryce actually loved playing mind games.

Our boys were only 12 and 14 years of age by this time, so one could not expect them to believe there was any truth in what they were hearing. They trusted and loved their dad. How could any man or woman bring their children into it to save themselves? So much for a loving dad!

Again, I decided to play dumb and let him believe that I trusted him. In the meantime, I hired a private investigator and tapped into his phone's message bank to expose him once and for all.

Looking back, I desperately wanted to hold our family together for the sake of our children, and I realise now I excused a lot of bad behaviour. But I was no fool. There comes a time where one has to face reality, have self-respect. This marriage was just never meant to be.

When I married Bryce, I truly loved him and I did not deserve what he had put our family through. I had given up so much at my age to have his children only to end up being hurt and alone as time went on. In fact, I remember telling Bryce I could never have children if I thought for one moment that I would ever be left to raise them on my own, as I had done before with my eldest children. He promised me that would never happen.

I was in Melbourne, and through my girlfriend, found a great private investigator in Brisbane who said he could help me. What I needed to do was get into his phone accounts and check the numbers he had been calling. It was proof I needed, so my boys would not turn against me even though I knew they would be devastated.

My behaviour was becoming addictive; needing to learn the real truth about this man. I was desperate to expose him for who he really was, wanted everyone that knew him to see. Bryce was just a coward, and I was prepared to do whatever necessary to get the truth. Suddenly, that was all that was important to me. I became obsessive.

John, my private investigator, went to great lengths to confiscate phone bills from the company my husband was working for at the time; quite illegal, but nonetheless, he did get the information I needed.

Not only had my husband been calling a woman named Deb in New Zealand in the very early hours of the morning, but he had also been calling Claire. You remember Claire? From Surfers Paradise, and who Bryce was involved with in the year 2000, and likely earlier. I had kept her number just in case, and all was about to be revealed by John, my private investigator.

That week, Bryce had a trip away, which was a good time to tap into his message bank. The trick was to put a new pin number in his phone and call him when he was in the air. It was perfect because I knew he wouldn't answer – that was the only time it would work.

The problem was, when he received any calls, I couldn't allow him to hear them, as I had already listened to them. No matter how important they were, I realised I would have to delete them, otherwise he would know that someone was tapping into his phone. When he landed, he would listen to his messages. Had I not deleted them, they would come up as saved messages, which would ultimately be telling him someone was listening. I could not take the risk of being caught.

I remember on his way back from a business trip, there was an American guy who left a message saying, 'Hi, Bryce. What the hell is going on? If you want my business, return my call'. This guy was so angry, he had left many messages and even though I knew his call was of great importance, it was more important for me to cover my tracks. So, again and again, I pressed delete.

Claire from Surfers rang him whilst he was on the plane and left a message to say she was vibrating in his pocket. That, I couldn't resist! Bryce returned home and I just glared at him and said, "Who is vibrating in your pocket?" He just stared at me; he couldn't understand how I knew. I left him guessing.

The time came to get in touch with my private investigator, John, who had asked me to call him at 5pm on the following Friday to give me the information I needed. I drove out to a quiet road and waited for his call. Strangely enough, I ended up at the same location my father had a very bad car accident when I was only eight years old.

Do I make the call now? It was an unbelievable feeling, and I will never forget that it was gut wrenching. But you know what, girls? It's about self-respect. Part of me did not want to know, while another part of me did. Well, it might sound silly but you know what I mean. I already knew, I just didn't know how many women there had been. I took a few minutes then made the call.

John answered and said, "I am so sorry."

Obviously, there was bad news.

Then he proceeded to tell me that my husband had made many calls in the middle of the night to New Zealand. While I realise now, there is a time difference between the two countries which would confuse me later. Then John said we have the same problem with another number being dialled to Surfers Paradise. Must have been hedging his bets!

Not only had Bryce been calling Deb in New Zealand in the wee hours of the morning, he had also been calling Claire.

He must have thought he was irresistible and was obviously deceitful to them as well.

I sat for some time in my car, so devastated that I couldn't even cry! What now? I drove home knowing that this was the end. It wasn't just about the calls; he had been travelling constantly and I knew he had been having affairs with these women.

It was time to face this lie I had been living for the past 22 years of my life. Yet all I could think of was that I was going to hurt my boys, and that was the most difficult decision I faced.

Nonetheless, it just couldn't go on. I had been such a fool, and wasted another 12 years from when he had left me in the first place. As far back as 1992—and even before we were married—I am sure he was cheating on me. I realise now I should never have taken him back, but I was the optimist looking for that family life I ached for and never had.

I arrived home trying for composure. Bryce was sitting in our home office.

Now what?

I approached him and told him that we needed to talk and asked him to go into the lounge. We only ever sat in the lounge when we had visitors or there was a special occasion as it was quite formal. I figured this was our last special occasion, the most appropriate place to end this farce of a marriage.

We sat across from each other; we were to attend a function that evening but I was the only one that would attend. I said to him, "I know what you have been doing."

"What do you mean?"

I then spelt out what I knew and, because he had no comeback, he knew he was done. It was over. It was such a short conversation, all over in a matter of minutes. It probably took longer to get married! While my anger had taken much to control, I had no reservations about what I had done. There was no going back. I felt humiliated as a person, just a joke. My whole life was destroyed in a few minutes and I couldn't comprehend what was to come.

My children were my prime concern, and I had asked Bryce not to tell them we were separating until the next morning.

I knew how upset they would be and I felt it far better that we told them together. It would still be painful, and I just wanted them to believe it was going to be amicable rather than nasty. It wouldn't make it less painful but they needed to know they still had both parents who loved them.

That did not happen.

Bryce had to get in first. That was who he was – selfish to the core. I should have guessed he would do that. He put a real spin on his version of the truth to our boys just like I expected him to do, brilliant manipulator that he was.

The next morning, my family was devastated to say the least. So much upheaval, the boys were crushed, and I felt they blamed me for destroying their family. Funny, after nearly seven years, I think they still feel the same way. Everything is always my fault or is it just me feeling guilty?

I felt my life was over, my dream for my family was gone – it wasn't going to be. Those 19 years of marriage had ended. What now? I had to face it like so many women and men do, just as I had done before. This time was different; I knew it was really over.

Bryce had slept the previous night in one of my son's bedrooms and left the following morning, not to be seen for some time. Just like he had disappeared in 1992. He really was a coward, and to this day, I cannot understand how any parent can just not care about how their children are coping. Bryce had become a heartless human being who only cared for himself. That much I knew about the man to whom I had devoted so many years.

I decided I needed to know more after I learned he had purchased a plane ticket to New Zealand, so I went back to the private investigator and had him followed. Yes, I had him followed. I wanted to know who she was and what she looked like. This was the only way to find out. I had become so obsessive, and didn't like behaving like this. While I should have taken the high road and not given it a second thought, I needed to know everything for my own peace of mind.

My private investigator, John, had connections with the FBI who were based in New Zealand and obviously had no cases that weekend. They got the call from John and proceeded to the airport in Auckland, New Zealand. I had sent a photo to John of Bryce, and it was passed on to the FBI.

The report goes like this:

OCTOBER, 2004
BRYCE [REDACTED]
FILE NO. [REDACTED]
INVESTIGATOR: [REDACTED]

1430	Commenced observations at Auckland International Airport.
1445	Flight [redacted] has landed and is processing.
1509	Subject exits the processing area wearing a white t-shirt, dark blue jeans and wheeling a large black suitcase.
1509	He is greeted by a female, description as follows: *Caucasian* *Aged in her 30s* *Approximately 5'6"* *Short hair, possibly a natural brown colour but highlighted blonde, styled in a spiked and dishevelled manner* *Slightly overweight* *Fair skin* *Wearing pink t-shirt, dark blue ¾ length pants and low black* *slip-on shoes*

1509	Subject and the female walk out of the terminal holding hands.
1509	They cross to the main car-park area and as they walk through the car park, the subject puts his arm around the female's waist.
1516	Subject places his suitcase into the boot of a red SS Commodore, registration number [redacted]. Both get into the vehicle with the subject driving and female in the passenger seat. Departs.
1528	Subject is using his cell phone while driving.
1548	Parks in Fort Street, Auckland city. Female departs the vehicle on foot and the subject sits and waits in the vehicle.
1550	Female returns to the vehicle and departs.
1611	Subject parks in Huron Street, Takapuna. Female away from the vehicle on foot and into *Shaver Shop*. Subject sits in the vehicle and waits.
1614	Female returns to the vehicle and departs.
1619	Parks Hurstmere Road, Takapuna, outside *The Copper Room*. *The Copper Room* is a popular bar, one of many situated in this area of Takapuna.

1619	Both get out of the vehicle and sit at a footpath table outside the bar. They order drinks and food, the subject drinking beer and the female white wine and they consume a plate of potato wedges.
	The subject and the female sit in chairs beside each other. Occasionally, during the course of their meal and drinks, the two would kiss briefly, and occasionally the subject would place his arm around the female's back in an affectionate manner.
1715	Subject enters the bar and uses the toilet and the female gets into the driver's seat of the Commodore.
1717	Subject exits the bar and female exits the vehicle. Both walk through the shops towards Takapuna Beach and walk along a reserve adjacent to the beach and return.
1753	Both into the red Commodore and to park with the female driving.
1758	Stops in Stratford Avenue, Milford, near the corner of Shakespeare Road. Subject gets out of the vehicle and crosses Stratford Avenue and onto Shakespeare Road. He goes out of sight to us for approximately 10 seconds then returns to the vehicle, gets into the passenger seat and they depart.
1805	Parks in the driveway of [redacted] Hogans Road, Glenfield.
1805	Female gets out of the vehicle, clears the mailbox and both then enter the house and go out of sight.
1805	[redacted] is a vehicle already parked in the driveway beside the Commodore. Three other vehicles are parked at the address but registration numbers are not visible.

1816	Commodore departs with the subject driving and female in the passenger seat.
1826	Parks at a block of shops at [redacted] Rosedale Road, Albany. The shops are known as Rosedale Park Village. The buildings in the complex are two levels with the downstairs level being shops and commercial premises and the upstairs levels, apartments.
1826	Subject removes his suitcase from the boot of the vehicle and both enter a doorway beside *Oriental Groceries* shop. A doorway provides access to an apartment upstairs. Upstairs windows have vertical Venetian blinds which are closed, preventing any view into the apartment.
1915	Stand down.

That's all I needed to confirm what I already knew; the end to the puzzle at last. John sent me photos of the two of them together. I have to say when I saw Deb, my first reaction was one of disbelief that Bryce would want such a woman. Very different. Devilish, for want of a better description.

Where to now? I had no idea. In a world of confusion, and left with the two boys he wanted so desperately. Interestingly enough, he really couldn't care less; what a complete bastard.

I actually phoned Deb not realising that the number I had found for her was her work number not her home. She didn't answer and I proceeded to leave her a message letting her know how disgusted I was that she had destroyed my family. She worked for Bryce in the New Zealand office and, unbeknown to me, her boss came to work that morning and heard the message. Bryce was horrified when he was called into the Melbourne office to be confronted by what was on the answering machine. Obviously, it didn't go down too well as this was one of his employees. Again, this is always where Bryce becomes unstuck – having affairs with his staff.

I don't know the excuse Bryce gave his superiors that day but I am sure he was inventive because Deb was the one who ended up without a job. He managed to hang onto his position for a while but in the end the inevitable happened, and he was out of work once again.

Rage at this whole situation had me decide to write a letter to Deb's husband. I had her address from the private investigator's report, and thought, *why should she get away with it?* Not that I placed all the blame on her but she knew he was married, and I had a low tolerance for women who went after married men.

My letter was direct and to the point. I gave him a detailed account of everything I knew that had taken place. It was a relief when I sent it without a return address. To this day, I don't know what happened to her or whether he ever received my letter.

Thinking back on this behaviour, it was no different from when I met Bryce 22 years prior. I had been working as a manager in a restaurant; Bryce came down one night and played the piano because his brother worked there too, which is how we met in the first place.

I was married at the time but it was not a good marriage; we had both been unfaithful to each other, and I think realised we were so young when we married. I was just 17 and my then-husband had just turned 19. We had grown in different directions although he did want to try to save our marriage but I had lost any feeling I had for him. More so after meeting Bryce.

If I was to be completely honest, I fell in love with Bryce after he pursued me for so long. I allowed it to happen so I suppose this is what they call karma. He didn't care that I was a married woman. Bryce went after whatever he wanted and there was no stopping him. He even befriended my husband at the time which I now feel is pretty low. I had experienced Bryce first-hand in that situation and never realised that was who he was. He liked the chase and he didn't care who he hurt as long as he won in the end.

I didn't feel guilty at first because my first husband drank too much and was a womaniser. Where I was lonely and looking for love. I was only 28 years of age and Bryce was there but much younger than me. He spoiled me, made me feel so special. Back then, you could say I was the selfish one. I didn't put my children from my first marriage before Bryce when I should have because I was so caught up in my own feelings. Love is a very powerful emotion that makes us do things we would not normally do.

I don't know whether Bryce just liked the chase or he was really in love with me in the beginning, or maybe it was that our boys were meant to be here. Who knows? It was just a relationship that should never have been.

There are so many regrets, but I am over punishing myself. We are who we are and we all make mistakes. I am very aware that I had many lessons to learn both through my own behaviour and the mistakes I chose to make, but I was a faithful person to Bryce for all those 22 years I knew him. For me, I had learned from my previous marriage that what I had done was wrong. It wasn't fair that my eldest children went through so much either, but I didn't desert them as Bryce did with ours.

Some of my friends had said to me to just turn a blind eye, that he would get past this behaviour, that I would still have a family. But what family?

How can you have a family knowing your husband or wife is continually cheating on you? What sort of marriage is that? Didn't I deserve better? The answer is: Yes, I did!

Lonely and devastated, with no one to turn to, I was on my own with two resentful teenage boys. To this day, I still do not understand any of this, or how I got to this point.

Now isolated, money was a problem. How would I keep my dream home?

I lived day by day, drank a lot, which I suppose was not the right thing to do, but it got me through each day and every night. So many years of my life had just been snatched from under me. I am not making excuses; that was just my reality. If I had known then what I know now, I would have been much stronger and coped far better with the situation. These days, I always keep top of mind: 'what does not break us makes us stronger'.

I still followed Bryce's movements. He had disappeared for a month, as he usually did, and didn't even contact his boys.

Unfortunately, during that time, my father passed away just a month after Bryce had left; even my father had continually asked where his son-in-law was. I just let Dad think Bryce was always on a business trip; I didn't want to upset him. My father died never knowing what had really happened. How much more was I supposed to go through?

There was nothing I could do for my dad as he was gone. My children became my focus, and I remember often wondering how anyone who calls themselves a parent, could do this. Children should be the priority; we bring them into this world, we have an obligation to see them through to adulthood and make their life a good one. It's obvious that with so many divorces, people in today's society just don't get it.

I had learned from my previous marriage the lessons I was meant to learn. Through my own experience, I see so much selfishness in parents now that put themselves continually before their children's needs. They think buying them things they don't need is okay, letting themselves off the hook, so to speak. The end result is that the children end up with the wrong values; they think it is okay. Society today is so destructive.

When I heard Bryce was going on an overseas trip, I just so happened to know the password for his credit card. I could follow his every move, and I did. It was clear that I was far from getting over what had happened, and I had to know more. His personality intrigued me.

I logged on as I did every morning and was just horrified to see he was off to America, which was the dream holiday he had planned for our family, but this was not to be. His companion was Deb from New Zealand, his mistress, who was married with a child. History was repeating itself; no different from when I had met Bryce. At one time, I was the married woman.

To those reading my story, I hope you see the significant lessons I had to go through to get to the other side. It happens to all of us who make mistakes. The lessons are real.

I was with Bryce and Deb every step of their trip, and became obsessed, watching everywhere they went. They had no idea. Not that it was fun but it did become obsessive, and it really wasn't something I should want to know, considering we were separated.

He spent a lot of money on Deb; I was just so devastated. Why wouldn't I be? This was the trip of a lifetime, one my boys and I should have taken with him, the trip we had spoken about so often, but that was not how it was. I had to move on but could not seem to stop myself from looking several times a day; it just made everything so much worse. It was an addiction I couldn't break.

When Bryce returned, I asked him about his trip and he denied it all, not knowing that I had watched his every move. What a liar! At the end of the day, what sort of person—a so-called devoted husband and loving father—could do what he had? It was all so surreal!

To this day, I still don't understand any of it, but I do often wonder if anyone really knows another? This happens in so many marriages. The only difference is that some try to protect their children. Not in Bryce's case. It comes down to whether you have integrity and honesty, whether you really have love for your children. I would like to think most of us want to protect those we love, and I had learned a lot by this time about myself and the mistakes I had made.

I still struggle watching my boys struggle with who their father really is, and why wouldn't they feel that way? They felt abandoned, no male mentor, no mate, no dad, no real sense of family.

Regardless, life had to go on, so I decided to sell the dream home. Fortunately for me, Bryce's guilt got the better of him and he let me have the house, which was one good thing that came out of it. It allowed me to try to start a new life, but it was the most difficult thing I have ever had to do. Remember, Bryce was just over eight years younger than me, and it was going to be harder for me to build another life.

I sold our home and moved to a rental. Funnily enough, *this* man that had given me our home had bought a townhouse in the same street. I couldn't believe it. He obviously had his own stash of money.

Out of 70,000 properties, we ended up in the same street. Mind you, he thought I had followed him, how wrong he was. How presumptuous of him! Why would I?

It was good for the boys that they could see their dad but that became a disaster as well. Bryce really did not want to see them at all. He put up with a couple of weekends here and there, and then nothing. The boys went through hell and back not understanding their father at all. They didn't say much to me at the time; they held it all in, but I knew they were having trouble dealing with the whole situation.

Bryce's life became about alcohol and women and, even though he had Deb and Claire, they didn't live in Melbourne.

I remember looking at his credit card account again to see what he had been up to and noticed he was bringing an unknown woman in from Canberra. With her name and flight details, it was obvious that she came from internet dating.

Even though we were not together, I had the urge to play private investigator. Not because I cared but I had started to enjoy the game. I think insanity had kicked in!

My girlfriend and I decided to dress up and go to the airport to see who this woman was. Gina was one of my closest friends and she thought it would be a laugh, so she went along with it. She dressed up in a burka and I wore a long black wig and clothes that I wouldn't normally wear. We laughed so much throughout the airport, it was ridiculously unbelievable.

We arrived at the terminal just in time to meet the plane. Deboarding had not started, and Bryce was nowhere in sight. We had the right details and it wasn't until I arrived home later that night that I noticed a charge on his credit card for the Hilton Hotel. She must have walked straight past us.

I have to say Gina and I had a great night; laughter is so good for the soul. Still, it was a bit insane. I should not have cared what Bryce was up to but I had to know everything... as I believe most of us do in this situation.

Then came Christmas, and Bryce asked our eldest son to join him on Boxing Day at a hotel with Deb, the woman he had been involved with all along. Our son did not know who she was until much later. When the penny dropped and he realised who she was, he didn't know how to handle the situation; he was only 15 years old.

His first thought was not to upset his father even though he felt himself becoming frustrated and angry with Deb, knowing she was his father's lover. He loved his father and did not want to alienate him in any way; he didn't want to lose him.

Worried and confused when he arrived home, he wasn't himself. He didn't want to tell me for fear I would be upset, and he was right. I was upset and angry. How dare Bryce put our son in a situation that was so confronting? That tells you the character of the man.

It was at that point I decided I would never look at Bryce's credit card again. I didn't want to know where he was or what he was doing. It was time to move on for the sake of our boys.

We didn't see much of Bryce after that. He was very rarely available to spend time with his children. The boys were still having problems and I knew I would be left to deal with them on my own.

Chapter 3

MOVING ON

Time moved on and I bought a home around the corner from Bryce. He had met a young woman named Jennifer on a plane; she was 33 and much younger than him. They fell in love and married two years later.

They moved to Brisbane in 2007 and married in 2009. Poor girl, I often wonder if she knew what she was in for. A leopard never changes its spots. My boys rarely saw their dad, although they stood up for him at his wedding. They just felt it was the right thing to do but it was far from the normal father-son relationship. If Bryce only knew what they really thought of him, he would be horrified. I am hoping that I have instilled certain principles and values in them and they would understand when they have families of their own, that they would never want to take after their own dad.

My girlfriend, Andrea, came to visit from Brisbane one weekend. In the early hours of the morning, I received a message on my mobile from an old friend of the family, his name was Brad. He was more a friend of Bryce's family, but he was very distressed; his ex-wife had just been killed in a car accident. I had known Brad for 25 years but couldn't understand why he was phoning me. We weren't at all close.

I returned his call about 4am on Sunday when I heard his message, and he was understandably very upset. We talked for a while and I told him I would call later that day to see if there was anything I could do, which I did.

It's funny how we all get caught up in other people's lives but I suppose it was another journey I had to take. One, I now feel, should never have happened.

Brad had two children who lived with him, he had always had custody and I had the upmost respect for him as a dad. Why wouldn't I? Considering I had been married to someone who was far from deserving of my respect.

Brad's children—a boy 9 and a girl nearly 13—were very close. I had no need to suspect he was someone I should never become involved with. No one in my family or friends ever liked him, not even my 80-year-old mother. They could see something I couldn't, and as my story unravels, it will become clear why their dislike was justified.

I asked Brad and his children for dinner a couple of weeks later. I knew he was going through a hard time and because of my compassionate nature, it was not uncommon for me to try and help a family dealing with grief. We had a lovely evening and caught up again the following week, and that is where I should have left well enough alone.

Coincidently, Brad was going to Surfers Paradise at the same time my boys and I were. We were staying at different hotels but still had arranged to catch up whilst we were there.

Before we left Surfers, Brad asked me out for dinner on our own and the kids all stayed back at my hotel, which should not have been a problem as my boys were older and able to keep an eye on the younger ones. Unfortunately, it didn't work out like that and it wasn't long after that they were fighting and we had to return to the hotel. I was angry with my boys but would come to learn later that Brad's son had a personality disorder. I should have walked away immediately because Brad did not recognise the behavioural problems in his child and continually brushed them aside.

After coming back from the Gold Coast, I didn't really think much of it. A few days had passed and Brad rang asking me to have dinner with him at his home. I didn't read too much into it – we were just friends. After that evening, I realised we were heading in another direction and I suppose because of my loneliness and vulnerability, I didn't want to listen to my family or my instincts.

We started seeing each other on a regular basis even though nobody in my family was happy. I didn't care because I was falling in love. It was all about that feeling.

When you have been hurt in the way I had been for so many years, one would think there could never be trust again but I looked up to this man because he was a real dad. What I had always wanted for my kids. I was not seeing anything clearly at all, just falling into another trap of despair and grief only to be hurt far worse in a shorter relationship than I ever had before.

Brad asked me to spend the weekend, so the boys and I went the first time together. However, it was a disaster again with all four kids. It wasn't going to work this way.

The following weekend, I selfishly went by myself and left my boys to take care of themselves. One was nearly 16 and the other nearly 18. I really thought they were old enough to start being responsible and look after themselves. It was time I should start having a life of my own but that was not to be the case.

I am sure you all have heard the old saying, 'when the cat's away, the mice will play'. Well, that was exactly what started happening. The underage drinking, the beginning of drugs, and the parties became a weekend event as I started to go to Brad's every weekend, leaving my boys in charge.

For some time, I wasn't fully aware that this was going on until it was bought to my attention by a neighbour. The boys seemed happy enough to have some space from me on weekends, so I never thought another thing about it.

Life with Brad and his children was really great to start with, until we decided to plan our first trip to Fiji with my boys. We had our own room and the kids had their room next to ours with an adjoining door.

It was Christmas, and everyone was getting along well. At least, I thought that was the case. Then one afternoon my boys took Brad's children to the pool, and that's where it all came undone.

Brad's youngest child, who was about 11 years old, started swearing at a toddler. My eldest son told him to stop it but he continued with the F word and the C word.

The child was around three years old, and the mothers sitting around the pool were horrified. So, my eldest son dragged Brad's son out of the pool and back to our room. I will never forget Brad's face; he was furious with my son. Nothing his son did was ever wrong. He was a child who put on an act, as if he was the one being hurt. Always the victim. My boys had young nieces and a nephew and knew the difference between right and wrong. They did not understand Brad's son's behaviour at all.

My son probably shouldn't have dragged him back to the room, but he couldn't get him out of the pool any other way, and wasn't hurting Brad's son as the child made out. It was all an act to get his father angry. If there is such a thing as a manipulating child, Brad's son was certainly it. After all, he had learned from the best – his own father. I couldn't understand why the mothers around the pool didn't report him.

Brad believed everything that came out of his son's mouth, so that was the end of the holiday. Brad was never the same after that. He blamed everyone except his son. I felt his son had a personality disorder or he was just a good actor.

I knew his mother had suffered with bipolar, which is a personality disorder; however, looking back, that was only what Brad told me. When I think on it, I now believe that maybe Brad was the one with bipolar.

The trip ended abruptly, and we returned home, leaving everyone unhappy. Not realising, I started blaming my boys for all the problems that arose, which was wrong. I wasn't seeing the real problem.

When we arrived home the next day, Brad called me and told me he couldn't see me anymore. I was devastated, and couldn't understand why he refused to get past what had happened and why. Did he not see what his son had done was so wrong?

A few weeks went by and I was miserable, but I knew I had to once again move on from this bad experience. That was difficult for me as I had become so involved with Brad. Then one afternoon he asked me to call into his home and see him, so I did.

He told me he couldn't be without me and we would make it work. Oh my God, where was my sense? It was all about that feeling! We started seeing each other again but this time it was different. I should mention that I came to realise that Brad was suffering from depression but, as I said earlier, I thought it could be bipolar. So, I became more involved and tried to give as much as I could to his family without question. Some people would describe my personality as a 'rescuer'.

I did the shopping every weekend expecting Brad to repay me when I returned, but when I asked for what he owed me, he would change the subject and, because of his delicate condition, I would drop the conversation. The money didn't seem important at the time, I just wanted to help him get better and I knew he would repay me one day – I trusted him.

You see, I had become his saviour, his lifeline, someone he depended on. Brad always said to me that he needed to get away and he would feel better if we could take a trip. So, I would make it happen. I took my saviour role seriously. He always asked me to take care of the bookings on my credit card and he would pay me back later. After many trips with Brad and his children, thousands and thousands of dollars later, I never saw the money. I was not the saviour, I was the fool!

To cut a long story short, I was totally in love with this man who I thought was my soul mate but he just continually took from me and, after nearly three years, I realised there was a problem. I had always been a giver, it was part of my nature, so I never saw a problem with it. It wasn't that he didn't have the money, he did, but I think his attitude was why use his money when he could use mine!

Brad's home, although a bit run down, was by a lake and he had all the good things in life including a beautiful boat, which was his pride and joy. So, I had no reason to suspect he would use me. His children were given everything they asked for; he was a bit over the top with them.

I think he was trying to make up for the loss of their mother, although I did not understand that either because she was, according to Brad, an abusive mother. It was why he had full custody. I continued down this destructive path thinking that he would make it up to me.

It didn't take long before I decided to sell from where I was living because Brad gave me the impression we should move in together. I should never have sold my home; it was a beautiful old house in one of the best streets in the city and Brad did not intend to move in with me. He just wanted me to have a good cash flow.

I didn't work that out for a while, but in the meantime, rented a lovely home overlooking the bay. I realise many of you reading this will be thinking how could anyone be so gullible? How could I allow anyone to use me like that? I never wanted for myself, only wanted to help everyone else. I had a 'people pleaser' personality and it certainly wasn't a good way to be.

Then one day he told me how nice it would be for me to have a townhouse on the water around the corner from him and, once his children were older, he would sell his home and move in with me. Then we would use his money to travel together, at least that was the plan according to Brad.

It all sounded so exciting and that's exactly what I did! I was due to move in the New Year but before that could happen we went on another holiday together with his son. Brad's daughter was an exchange student overseas in France, and my boys wouldn't think of going away with him. They could barely tolerate Brad and were no different from the way the rest of my family felt.

I should mention that earlier one of my friends found him on a dating service on the internet. He told me it was all a joke and one of his ex-girlfriends had placed him on it, and I believed him. You would think I would have learned by then, particularly after what I had been through with Bryce.

Brad and I had broken up three times in the course of nearly three years. I had bought my new home and looked forward to living around the corner from him. The telltale signs of who he really was were always there. He had always been a very selfish lover in the bedroom; he was a real taker. Why didn't I ever get it? It should have been my first clue, and he certainly wasn't a good lover.

I should have known; after all, he was the only man I had ever been with since I was 17 years of age, that had never given me an orgasm. Yes, a very sad sexual existence for any woman! Brad was only interested in himself and what he could get out of any given situation.

It's funny when I think about it, but Bryce was the best lover I had ever had. Even after everything we had been through, I knew that was not the reason for his continual affairs and I did really miss that.

We went off on our holiday to Cairns. At Brad's insistence, I booked and paid for it because he was always too busy and depressed. Again, what a fool I was!

That holiday was our last. However, I am sure he knew that and used me one last time.

If only I had of seen the movie *He's Just Not That Into You*. Maybe I would have got it earlier and it would have saved me a great deal of heartache and money. Looking back, I was unconsciously buying affection; maybe I had no self-esteem. I think Bryce had taken that from me after seeing the type of women he had been with.

I don't think Brad or his son would have missed me if I wasn't at the resort with them; they spent every moment together, leaving me to amuse myself. Not that I was jealous of the time he gave to his son, it's just that it was not a normal man-woman relationship. There was no balance, and to me, his relationship with his son was just a bit over the top.

Our relationship was more that of siblings, or someone just along for the ride. He did not appear to be in love with me at all.

I suppose if he had been a gorgeous-looking man, maybe there would have been good reason for me to feel the way I did but I never took any notice of people's looks. He was overweight and always dressed like a slob but that didn't matter to me; I was in love with him... or at least I thought I was. It's all about that feeling, that's what gets you hooked.

When I reminisce, I think I admired the dad in him – he was always so attentive to his kids despite not always doing the right thing by them, which became sickening after a while, realising he was not who I thought he was.

In other words, allowing and encouraging bad behaviour. There were many incidences that horrified me that I haven't spoken about in this book, so maybe that was not really being a good dad in the first place. His daughter was not like her brother; she was always a remarkable young woman for whom I had a lot of time.

Often, Brad encouraged his son's bad behaviour. I remember on one occasion the boy started taunting one of their neighbours in a very deceptive way. She was a single mother who had two girls and really did nothing wrong. Brad's son would swear at her and her girls, and he would always go home to his father with a different story, one that only grew hostility in Brad.

After this had been going on for some time, the neighbour took a restraining order out on Brad's son and they ended up in court where I was prepared to be a witness for this lie as I had only seen what he wanted me to see. He was a very manipulative boy, and to this day I believe he had a problem that his father was not aware of. I decided to find out more about the situation and I realised that Brad's son was making the whole thing up just to get his father's attention. I was so sorry for the woman and her girls who lived only a couple of doors from him.

Sometimes, things are not what they seem, so I am very careful these days not to get involved in anyone's problems. Brad's son was a nightmare and I had no idea that he was so manipulative. In the end, they had intervention orders out on each other and when I really thought about it, why would any sane parent allow their child to swear and abuse a neighbour, or anyone for that matter?

Brad had taken such advantage of me, I was devastated and felt violated that another human being could blatantly lie and use me in the way he had. Bryce was bad enough but he never drained me financially. To me, this was so much worse. For nearly three years, I lived a complete lie. For 27 years, his friendship was a lie too.

He was obviously never a friend. In fact, I don't think he ever knew what real friendship was. Brad was, and is, a user of people. Someone I didn't want in my life, and was so glad to be rid of.

There were so many clues I should have noticed when I was with Brad. Obvious ones. Once again, I was in love with being in love, although I did always think of us as friends first. The thing is, real friends would never think of using or hurting you in that way. It was all premeditated. He knew exactly what he was doing in a relationship with me. I should have known a few months before Brad ended it when we were talking about living together and his son turned around in front of him and said, "Suz, my dad will never live with you!"

Yet another clue! He was only 11 years old at the time and Brad never said a word. He just looked away as if he did not hear what came out of the boy's mouth. When I approached him later about it, he said I was paranoid and his son didn't know what he was talking about.

Like father, like son. They were both manipulators. I know that sounds awful saying that about a child but Brad had taught him to be that way.

Even when we were away on holidays, we all went jet skiing and Brad told his son to leave his hired vest on under his jumper and walk out with it. I was horrified, to say the least. How could anyone teach his or her child to steal?

I made him take it back, and from that point on, I was the bad person. They just didn't get right from wrong. That's another time I should have known that they were dysfunctional.

We arrived back from what was to be our last holiday together then went our separate ways. Brad didn't say much to me but I knew something was brewing. I was going away the following week with all my children and grandchildren. Brad and his son were to join us mid-week in a holiday spot called Yarrawonga, and even though all four of my children could not stand him, they had accepted he was part of my life.

I had seen him the weekend prior and he was quite cool to me, even in bed, not that I was missing anything. My instincts were telling me there was a problem. What I didn't realise was that the problem would be no different than what I had experienced in my marriage. The man I fell in love with was no different to the man I married but to me, Brad was much worse. He was false! Brad had bled me dry financially and emotionally in such a short time. He separated me from my own family, and the only way I can describe it is to imagine if you were involved with a religious cult. Manipulation. That word comes to mind so often when I think about Bryce and Brad!

I left for my holiday and Brad said goodbye to me; he would be up during the week so I thought maybe his change of personality would blow over but that was not to be.

Mid-week came and I hadn't heard from him, with the exception of me calling him to let him know I had arrived safely in Yarrawonga. I tried calling him a couple of times but there was no answer. Then I received a text. Yes, a text! I had given this man everything for just on three years. I cleaned his house every weekend, nursed him back to health through his deep depression, did his shopping, fed his family, took him on holidays, looked after his children, drove him to his counselling sessions, and I received a text to say he just wanted to be friends. I couldn't believe what a fool I had been.

I feel embarrassed writing about it, telling the world I am a first-class fool.

The upside—and yes, there is an upside—is that I have learned my lesson in life. Finally. Which is not to be so giving, and if a man is not even giving in bed don't let him use you. I often wonder if we ever really know anyone, we come into this world alone and go out of it alone; it's what we attract into our lives that makes a difference. Life is just full of lessons, and it seemed I had so many to learn.

On my return, Brad wouldn't even see me. I would email him and text him, telling him I just wanted and needed closure. I asked him to return the money he owed me for all the holidays and shopping but nothing came. Then one day I was talking to a friend who also lived on the water nearby, and she told me that she had seen him with a woman; tall, long dark hair and with children. She had seen them quite often on his boat whilst I was away in Yarrawonga.

Later, I learned he had met this woman the previous year. Her name was Sandra. Her son went to school with Brad's son, and she had made visits to his home on several occasions with her three boys.

I never thought anything of it as she had a partner, and

I did not feel threatened by her in anyway, although she was 15 years his junior.

It was then I realised I had been taken for another ride. How very sad it is that some people find it so easy to hurt others. After all, how do these people live with themselves and their deceptions?

Brad was involved all along with another woman. I knew something was wrong when his personality changed. It is a sure giveaway that something—or someone—is going on.

Much like when I was with Bryce: when a man changes, you can be sure that there is somebody else.

Obviously, I had not learned my lessons when I was with Bryce. I have come to believe that if we don't learn those lessons the first time, we go through it all over again.

Chapter 4

ISOLATION

It was a downhill spiral from that point. I started drinking and I was still smoking; I had taken it up again when I was with Brad. It was worse knowing I had to move near him in a few weeks, and I was not up for it. Couldn't get my head around what had happened. Why was I such a fool? Those feelings of betrayal, both financial and emotional, I couldn't get past them. What was wrong with me? Why was I never good enough? I felt worse than I did when Bryce cheated on me for all those years, and I was alone again.

My family and friends were all so happy Brad was gone forever. They were over the moon. Everyone I knew was delighted. However, I could not understand why they didn't have any compassion for what I had been through. I was so miserable and lost.

Looking back, I now understand why they all felt that way. I wasted so much time pining after someone that was clearly not worthy of me. They could all see who Brad really was when I was so blinded.

I moved into my new home and, although very unhappy, I got through it. What we don't realise when we are going through matters of the heart, is that our children suffer because of our behaviour, which can be said about many on the same path.

Maybe that is why our society and teenagers are different today? I do blame a lot of it on divorce and the change in family life. There are so many more single mothers and fathers raising children on their own with no help from their spouses. That alone can bring on depression and changes in behaviour. Mental health in today's society is a serious issue that should be a priority to our government.

Those that have gone through a similar situation, I am sure would agree when I say, one becomes oblivious to anyone else's problems when going through the aftermath of a relationship. It may sound selfish but it is not intentional. That is just how it is.

My boys had been through enough; they did not need more heartache around them. They had enough to cope with their dad living in Brisbane and living with a mother who drank a lot. I was just adding to their problems. The boys started going out a lot. This made me feel so alone and very isolated. I had cut myself off from most of my friends when I was with Brad; that's the way he liked it. In saying that, no one actually liked him.

My eldest children, now grown with their own children, had never been a problem through the difficult years when I was going through the divorce with their father. Yes, they had issues, but they dealt with them. At least, I thought they had until years later. The problems I faced with the younger boys, even though they were 16 and 18 at the time when I was living around the corner from Brad, were horrendous. I really believe that it was not just about our own situation but the change in society. The easy access to drugs and alcohol was the downfall of many young people.

There were so many problems. I remember thinking, *am I ever going to live through it?* Loneliness and isolation were bad enough, but the behaviour I had to deal with was intolerable.

I felt guilty for moving so much over the past six years and not giving our children the stability I should have. There was no help from their father, Bryce. I had to find a way back to sanity for all of us.

Drugs, drinking, and parties bought on anger and depression but thankfully, my boys were never in trouble with the law.

Don't get me wrong, they were loving kids, but I could see the effects of what the divorce had done to them, particularly because their father was not around to support them. Boys, no matter how old, look to have a relationship with their dad. I blamed Bryce for not doing that.

As I said previously, my dream when they were born was to give them a loving, stable home not put them through a divorce, broken relationships, and hostility. I say again, I will never understand how any parent can just forget they have children, no matter how old they are.

Bryce maintained he was a great dad but really, he was an absentee father who was oblivious to what we were going through.

It was the hardest journey I travelled, watching my boys suffer emotionally. The eldest was the worst. I do feel he carries insecurities as I mentioned earlier when he chased his father's car down the road after Bryce left the first time when only four years old. I am sure he remembers that awful, emotional time in his life. My efforts to get him to see a psychologist have not borne fruit because he feels he is okay. But he is not okay; he has anger issues, and if not addressed, he will carry them with him for the rest of his life.

We dealt with the issues as they arose, and life seemed to be a continual struggle for me and for them. I got lonelier and lonelier and started gambling, which was another bad choice. Loneliness can drive you to many places, and the pokies were where lonely people went.

I got to know who they were and why they were at the pokies every week. The same expressionless faces would always be sitting in front of a machine. I know many people would not understand this situation, that we should be in control of our feelings, and rightly so, but no one has the right to judge others unless they can walk in the same shoes and feel what they are feeling. Loneliness is a state of mind and many have to work through it, just as I did.

In my opinion, bringing pokies into our communities was one of the worst decisions our government has ever made. It was never in the best interest of families and communities. It preys on vulnerable people, and only makes their situation much worse.

The government, whether communities realise it or not, has a lot to answer for.

In fact, many families today are so dysfunctional because of our government. Families have changed. I am sure many of you will remember the '50s, '60s and '70s when the family was so different. I feel we were the fortunate ones. We didn't have hotels closing at 5am, kids out of control, many more people killed because of drink driving, much more violence on our streets, children exposed to internet bad behaviour and pokies bleeding the vulnerable financially dry, which led to many children suffering because of it.

I don't mean to take responsibility away from those that choose this way of life. Governments have to realise that the decisions they make for communities change the behaviour of those that are struggling with mental health; depression is a huge mental health issue.

Let's take violent video games and movies, for example. What are children now learning at a young age? They are learning how to be violent, and if they don't see it in their own home, they see it in someone else's. Surely, there are people out there like me who think the same way. I believe I have the authority to speak out on this subject because I raised children in the '70s and again in the '90s onwards.

I have seen first-hand the huge shift in our society and yes, I blame the government for playing a huge role in the demise of families.

Chapter 5

CONTINUING THE JOURNEY

I realised I was spending too much time alone, spending too much money in the pokies. It was time to stop feeling sorry for myself.

It is not worth throwing your life away for any man or woman. I was being pathetic. Therefore, six months later, I sold my property and moved back to my hometown. I had lost a lot of money through stamp duty on properties I had bought. It was time to make changes for the sake of my children and myself.

I went into real estate for six months and realised I was not going to make enough money to survive being on a retainer, always having to pay the company back every time I made a sale. So, I needed a better income; I still had one of my boys at school waiting to go onto university, and I needed to help him pay for his costs.

Bryce, their father, cut them both off financially when they turned 18 and would not help with education or anything else after that. It is a very difficult situation for a lot of single parents and young people today with no support. I realise many kids have put themselves through university but every year gets harder and harder for young people to survive with every-day living costs. That is why we have homeless teenagers, who have no support, all around the world.

Our education system is to blame for so many kids not fulfilling their dreams because some don't get into university if they don't get the required score for the end of year 12. I am of the belief that a pass should be enough, and they still should have the opportunity and be accepted into one of our universities. What is the alternative for them? Nowhere!

What Bryce refused to realise, had we been together, he would have gladly paid for his son to finish his education but he had a new wife and I don't think she approved of him paying for anything. I have to say I think she is a good person, it's just that she had been bought up at a young age to be self-sufficient and felt all young people should be the same. She was probably right in many ways but every family has different circumstances, and opportunities do not always come along for young ones as they used to. We live in a very different world today. Bryce and his wife could afford to offer some support to the boys. After all, they certainly could afford it they had two homes – one in Brisbane and one in Melbourne.

My resentment toward Bryce was still there. For a long time, I felt he had the better life, no responsibility at all. A life where he only had to worry about himself. I call it a very selfish life, one that he would regret in the years to come as he gets older. He will have no memories of his sons' birthdays, getting their driving license or the many Christmas's he missed, along with the every-day connection a dad has with his sons and their mates.

Maybe one day he may understand that his selfishness was never worth the heartache he put us through. So much damage was done.

It is six years now since that awful day when our family fell apart, and it has been a real struggle for me to maintain my mental health. Nobody knows how I feel; only those that are going through or have experienced a similar situation would understand.

I know some people would say I was weak and you don't need a man, but that is not true for many. It takes time to understand our journey, and for everyone it is different. I think a lot of it comes from your upbringing and the insecurities within yourself.

Not only did I have to deal with my own sanity raising two teenage boys, but also with behavioural issues caused by drugs and alcohol. I am sure there are many parents that have had to deal with similar issues and know that drugs are the worst thing that can happen to a family. Finally, my boys are getting on with their lives and realise the emotional rollercoaster they put us all through, although they still have their moments.

I would not wish these feelings on my worst enemy, and that is just what they are – 'feelings'. I have learned over the past six years through reading so many wonderful self-help books, that feelings can be changed so quickly. You just have to know how.

Turning a negative into a positive; feeling sad and then happy. It really is not necessary to go through all the pain and the struggle with the isolation and feeling of loneliness.

I realise that now, and maybe our kids from a very young age should be taught about emotional and financial survival; as I said, it is all about emotions. We all have a choice. We need a program in our schools that may help many young people to learn about life skills. It could make the world of difference learning about coping mechanisms. It may help in the prevention of young people committing suicide. I wish I had known how to cope with difficult situations when I was younger. Perhaps, I would have handled what happened to me differently. I suppose many think it just comes naturally. Maybe so, but for many it is difficult and depends a lot on mental stability.

This is where I am right now.

Trying to turn sadness into happiness. Taking control of my feelings. I had decided to find a business I could put all my energy into, something of interest to me. Something different, because I had come to believe if I am happy, everyone around me would be happy. More importantly, I needed to get my life back.

Where do I begin? How do I reinvent myself? I had no idea how to go about this, and had never felt so out of control with who I was but I knew I had to forge ahead. Otherwise, I would not survive.

I must have applied for over 100 jobs, and I knew first-hand how frustrating and horrible it was when you put your heart and soul into your applications only never to hear from most employers.

Nobody cares who you are, and even though I had an excellent resume, it was so difficult to find employment. Then one day, my accountant said to me if I didn't get a job then I needed to buy a business otherwise I was going to go broke.

The penny dropped!

The search was on. The first thing I needed to do was list my interests, the things that made me happy. So, I did.

I narrowed it down to restaurant, café, or hairdressing and beauty. I loved making people happy, making them feel good about themselves. So after months of agonising over where I was meant to be, I decided on hairdressing even though I was not a hairdresser. I was interested in beauty so I started searching the internet – day after day for months, looking for the right business. I had limited finances and knew whatever I chose, I had to have the confidence to carry it through. This was my last chance.

With hairdressing and beauty, I thought I could manage the business and perhaps take some courses in make-up and beauty to extend it. All my family warned me not to go down this track; they had no confidence in my ability even though I knew my marketing skills would be invaluable to any business. I had to trust myself and not worry about what anyone said. If it was going to be, it was up to me. That was what I told myself every day.

Sometimes, it is good to run business or personal ideas past your family and friends but it is not for everyone. It can stop you from moving forward; too many opinions can bring mistakes.

I had never had a problem making business decisions. In fact, it was the one area of my life that I was always confident about. I worked in media, marketing, business development, property management and had been a Councillor in local government for six years. There was no reason to feel I could not make it in any business, but due to my bad relationships, my self-confidence had been destroyed.

It reduced me to feeling bad about who I was. For the first time, I had no confidence in any area of my life. I was running on empty, and wasn't interested in another relationship. That was not the answer for me. I just wanted to become free and financially independent. When I say, free at the age of 56 even though I had applied for many jobs, I wasn't sure I could actually work for anyone ever again. I needed to find a business I could manage and have the freedom I yearned for, which is why I decided on hairdressing and beauty.

Beauty has always been a huge industry all around the world, but more so now in the 21st century. So, after giving it a lot of thought, I concluded this was where I needed to be. As I said previously, I thought I had the marketing skills to grow a business.

No one agreed with me but I was not going to allow anything or anyone to hold me back. My biggest fear was that I would end up homeless, and I had to remove that thought because I always believed what we think about we bring about. I still had my son to put through university without any help from his father, so I had to make it work. I had to be sure.

Chapter 6

IN SEARCH OF HAPPINESS

I continued to search the internet for a good salon that was within my budget, while at the same time submitting appropriate job applications on a daily basis to cover all my bases. On top of that, I had also bought a townhouse off the plan and expected it to be finished by this time but it hadn't even started. So, I was in a very delicate financial position but continued to look at the bigger picture. I knew I had to make the right move to secure a good future.

In the meantime, I looked at all opportunities—big and small—while concentrating on better health. I knew that if I lost weight and gave up all my addictions, I would gain confidence and be ready to take on the world.

Months went by and I came across a great salon in a place called Malvern. The owner had been there for 17 years and the rent was low. It was a great location and I believed this to be the one because it was so established. My eldest son from my first marriage kept telling me I was wrong and he talked me out of it, said I was far better off going into a restaurant because I had so much knowledge of them. I wanted the salon because it meant

I could keep my home I was building; I could have both as the hair salon was less money. In the end, I suppose I didn't trust myself and believed in what he was telling me. After all, my background was critiquing restaurants and writing editorial for them. It had been 28 years since I had actually managed a restaurant but I also knew it was the happiest time of my life.

My eldest son, who had been a psychiatric nurse for 14 years, wanted a change of career and aspired to becoming a chef, much to my surprise. I know now this was the real reason he talked me around. He wanted to come into the restaurant with me and live his dream, although now looking back, I am not sure now that was his dream. I think he watched too many *Master Chef* shows. He later realised it wasn't as easy as it looked.

We came across a restaurant that was more expensive than I had planned on buying but he kept on encouraging me to take the risk. My mum and I drove down to the restaurant and decided I was right – it wasn't a good location. Again, my son made me feel like most men did, that I could not make good decisions. So, I gave in and bought it.

Jack, my son, was so excited and I didn't want to let him down. Several times I felt like pulling out of the deal, but he continually gave me confidence to succeed and kept moving forward. Once again, I should have listened to my instincts! He kept telling me how proud he was of me making the right decision. As I felt I had let him down when I left his father, I was making a decision based on emotional thoughts.

My daughter and youngest son kept telling me it was a mistake and would end up ruining our family. How right they were!

It is really hard being a mum when you are trying to please everyone, but I had to move forward and without Jack, I don't believe I would have had the courage to do that.

In saying that, I was not in a good emotional place to make such a big decision.

It was funny that he used to be the negative one; it was almost as if we had changed places. I used to be the positive one but after my failures in relationships, I had lost all confidence in making the right choices but with Jack's help, we were starting to move forward and regain the confidence I once had.

My younger boys were still a problem and still angry with the world. One in particular, but I had no control over them so I had to learn to let go. I thought by being away from them for long periods whilst I worked would encourage them to grow up. My youngest was 19 years old and was starting to put his life together but the other was still struggling to find himself at 21.

Having a second family and being alone had nearly destroyed me, and I knew it had to change. My eldest two children had never really been a problem; they were living on their own at 18 and were more self-sufficient. This says a lot about our society; after all, they all had the same mother and all were touched by divorce. Although, I still felt I had done something wrong to cause them to feel the way they did. If I am to be entirely honest, my mistake was giving them so much, thinking I was making it up to them for not having a dad. So, yes, I am to blame for that.

I hoped the restaurant would bring my family closer together, bring me the financial independence and freedom of which I had dreamt. Always a believer in the books I had read, *The Secret* and *The Law of Attraction* were two of my mainstays. Although I had not lived by their teachings, just the opposite, which is why maybe everything seemed to go wrong up to that point in my life.

To be successful, one needs to have a positive outlook and not fear the worst. I knew that I had to change and so I told myself every day that my life was changing for the better. Kept up my mantra: if it is to be it's up to me.

The restaurant was going to be my saviour, my sanity, my freedom. At this point, I was not interested in having another relationship. All I wanted was financial freedom, to prove to myself I could do it and was prepared to work harder than I had ever done before.

The restaurant was across the road from the beach on the beautiful peninsula. It was a café during the day and restaurant with a touch of class by night. Over the years, I had been involved in marketing and had managed a restaurant 28 years prior, so I was hoping it would be like riding a bike and would all come back to me. It did. Making the decision to buy the business nearly drove me crazy. I was for it one minute and backing off the next. It was not an easy decision to make.

I realise now when you feel that way, you should not make decisions. That is your instinct telling you that you are making a mistake. I had very little confidence in myself, and I understand why after looking back.

How I allowed men to treat me had made me into a person I didn't even recognise, but once I signed on the dotted line it was full steam ahead.

Jack, my son, started his apprenticeship and was so excited. Here was a man nearly 39 years of age starting a new career, which I thought was rather courageous, but he loved to cook and he was able to fulfil his dream.

We finally took over, and I just knew that *finally* I had made a good decision! One that would enhance my life, get me out of being a recluse and give me financial freedom. It wasn't just about money; it was knowing I could still help my children when they needed. Once I got the business to where I wanted it to be, it would give me the freedom to travel. It's really important when we get to a mature age that we know it's our time, and sometimes it is not possible to experience the joys of life that we wish for but always remember we have to make it happen.

I knew it would be a life change, and it was the hours and the stress of having more responsibility than I had ever had in my life... with the exception of raising children twice on my own.

My life was finally moving forward to a stage where there was always light at the end of the tunnel. I had rid myself of my addictions, although I still had the occasional drink but never had another cigarette or gambled ever again. That was a challenge, but I did it.

As I have said previously, don't ever criticize anyone for having addictions because we are all guilty of having something addictive in our life. We can only encourage and try to help those that want to break free from their own addiction.

Chapter 7

WHAT I HAVE LEARNED?

Where do I begin? There have been so many lessons. Some I had to learn over and over again, particularly when it came to the type of man I was attracting and the neediness I had to overcome.

My lessons were actually just about me, how to believe in myself and be courageous making life-changing decisions, to take a leap of faith. Not to judge others and certainly not to wear my heart on my sleeve for the world to see.

I always thought I needed a man to make me happy, and didn't realise happiness was within; although, I still think it's wonderful if you are one of the lucky ones who have found your life-partner because I never believed we were meant to go through life on our own.

My life should have been different, and it would have been had I not lived with so many insecurities as a child. Still, like so many families in those days, my parents knew no better. They did the best they could. Again, what we learn from our parents, many of us carry through our lives. It is simply the bad behaviour of our parents through generations, instead of learning by their mistakes and having the insight to change the patterns, because that's exactly what they are.

I feel my journey has been so infected by the side-effects of growing up in an alcoholic family. Rather than changing the pattern, I continued down the same destructive path. I blamed everyone and everything around me for my bad choices, so I always had an excuse.

When I look back now, I was a fearful child, a scared child. All I ever wanted was to feel safe and secure in a happy home where there were no conflicts. Even growing up, I was a teenage alcoholic but didn't realise it. A binge drinker is an alcoholic, and I was just a child at 13 years of age.

I think being married at 17 and having a baby did not help; in fact, I believe it was the beginning of the end.

My first marriage had its ups and downs, but I did not realise how important it was to me until it was over, but isn't that always the way? Another lesson is to never take anything for granted, and that the grass is never greener on the other side. I love that saying because it is so true, and I am sure many of you would agree with that from your own experiences.

Alcohol plays a huge, destructive part in many people's lives and they don't even realise it.

It affects the way we think, our emotions and, so importantly, our decision making. It is great if you can go through life and have no regrets. I have so many, I would not know where to start!

Many of my lessons came from making the wrong choices; not just because of alcohol but also attracting the wrong partners in my life. I never knew how to listen to my instincts but now I am finally learning.

The biggest lesson I have learned is to stop depending on anyone else to make my life right – I have to do it myself. I realised I had to complete this journey with my children in the best possible way. To be a great role model and to show them that if I can make a success of my life, then they could as well.

I suppose this is mainly for my younger boys, not so much my eldest son and daughter from my first marriage. I was proud of them up to that time. They would have their own lessons to learn in life and I had hoped they had actually learned from my mistakes. However, today's youth, a different generation, had not just alcohol but drugs to deal with everywhere they go. So, my work was really cut out for me. I just had to make them realise they could have a better life than what they experienced with me.

I am not saying I was a bad mother because I was not. I did the best I could under my circumstances.

Now, I have the opportunity for myself and that's what the next half of my life is about – to work hard, earn my own living, be responsible for my own happiness, respect who I am and believe that my kids are proud of me and who I have become.

Chapter 8

MY BIGGEST LESSON

A couple of months in, the restaurant had gone by and it was a struggle. I had bought in a seasonal location without realising that it was like a ghost town in the winter.

I had received all the financial information before I bought the restaurant and I thought I had followed all the right procedures when purchasing a business. My accountant had looked at the figures the owner had provided; a legal document as proof of financials.

Yet, I was so oblivious to the fact that the previous owner had lied, and not just about the figures he had provided. He had made the chef part of the contract and all the staff said they would stay on. Unfortunately for me, I learned later he had told his staff that I was going to sack them all. He had several other businesses that he needed them to work in and moved them around to the different locations for his catering business on a weekly basis.

I was left with a shell. No chef and no staff.

It was time to start again. Here I was in another crippling situation. I couldn't believe it, and was devastated once again. I had put everything I had into the restaurant, even the money I had saved for my home.

There was no other choice but to be really strong and make the restaurant work, otherwise I was going to end up with nothing. Once again, I felt ripped off. Why was this happening to me? I knew why. Because I didn't trust my own decisions and listened to my son, Jack.

The money was running out quickly. Even though I had hired a new chef and new floor staff, we were not doing much business because it was winter and I kept telling myself I had to make it to the spring and summer, which is when the business would become viable. This was a seasonal restaurant.

In the midst of all of this, my son decided he did not want to be a chef, which once again devastated me. He was a big part of the reason I bought the business. I remember having cold feet many times but he always encouraged me. I am not blaming him entirely, as this was my decision and I had to face the consequences.

Chapter 9

FAMILY DISASTER

My son went back to his job as a psychiatric nurse. Fortunately for him, he could do that, but I thought he would still help me out. His wife was reconciling the books and some other office work for me but it didn't take long for me to realise they both virtually walked away from me and left me to go through this enormous strain on my own.

The arguments in the family started, and I saw a side to my eldest children I had not seen before. A selfish side.

Here I was, struggling to survive on my own and the only people who supported me were my nieces.

They were two beautiful girls who offered to work for me for nothing. Not only were they beautiful, they were amazing young women who have taught me the real meaning of family. They had lost their father to cancer some years previously and said to me when you lose someone you love it makes you more compassionate and considerate to any family situation.

Families become more precious!

My family was broken in a way I had never experienced. My eldest son and his wife had deserted me, and that hurt more than anything. It's true what they say, never go into a business with family. I should have listened to that because I felt so cheated.

I was not giving up. Things were getting to a point where I felt like I was living just day to day. I had to get through it, and all I could think about was getting to spring and hoping for better weather when people would actually want to go out. It had been the worst winter for 15 years that we had known, and I had to stay strong with no sign of relief in sight.

There was no other choice but to put the restaurant back on the market. I was doing most shifts by myself with the exception of Friday and Saturday nights, trying to keep the costs down. I was even laundering the napkins, tea towels, and doing all the cleaning of the restaurant. I had to save on costs. It was the only choice I had. My body was feeling the effects. Sometimes, I could hardly walk.

I just prayed every day that the restaurant would sell even as the days and nights grew longer and longer. "If only," I would say to myself on a daily basis. If only I had not been so naïve. Why couldn't I make the right choices? Why and how did I end up in this mess? Why did I buy a business in a town that was a holiday destination? It was so isolated and the locals did not support their restaurants. My eldest sister had also warned me she hated this small town for her own reasons.

Yet, I couldn't dwell on it; I felt like I was going crazy and money was running out fast, my family was dysfunctional and I only had myself to blame. It was my decision regardless of any encouragement I received from my son. I just kept praying that I would sell the restaurant and come out on top. This whole experience had taught me the value of money and the importance of keeping a job. These last six years of my life had been a nightmare, one I just wanted to move on from. To start again. If I just kept the money I got after the sale of our family home, I would have been fine and could have lived off the interest.

I really would not have needed to work had I done it right. In hindsight, it sounds great, but in reality, who knows?

I wanted to completely wipe the slate clean and start making good choices for my life, find a good job. At my age, I knew that was going to be difficult... keeping in mind I had put in for over 100 jobs in the last year before I had bought the business, which was another reason that I looked for a business in the first place.

Spring was fast approaching and I was not feeling well. Every bone in my body ached. The chef was right; it was a young person's business, not for someone who was nearly 60 years of age. With the stress of it all, I took up smoking again.

Alone and horrified of what was to become of me, I kept going. Spring was almost here. At the same time, I was trying to keep a positive approach. My mother had always been a strong force in my mind not to give up. She was an amazing woman who didn't depend on anyone. She always had so much faith, and I knew I had to be more like her.

It's not that I didn't believe in who I was at that time; I just felt broken and started questioning why this was happening to me and what was the lesson this time I was supposed to be learning? I tried always to do the right thing by others, but sometimes that was no benefit. As wrong as that may sound, I felt as if I was being punished, and for what?

It had come down to the crunch; it was only two weeks to September school holidays and I was down to nothing financially. I knew the weekend would either make or break me and on top of that, three of my best staff were off. It couldn't get any worse.

I had to stay strong even when my body was telling me to give up. Never had I felt those aches and pains before. Not like this. My weary hands and legs had to make it.

Still battling with the betrayal of my son and his wife, which was really getting to me, I knew nothing was going to change if I didn't. I just had to get on with it on my own and stay focused. There were a couple of nights when we would pick up on the weekends, and I remember my niece telling me to call my son and his wife and ask them to come in to help, but they wouldn't even do that despite knowing I was desperate.

It was always my belief that families were there through thick and thin to support each other in times of need but not in my case. I was angry all the time yet knew that what I was feeling was not going to get me anywhere. I was alone and that was how it was, I had to accept it. There was no knight in shining armour to help me. Nor was there going to be.

I still questioned why my past relationships that infected my life to begin with were doing so well. Bryce and Brad seemed to have it all. I couldn't understand why I was the one who had to go through what I called hell.

They had their relationships and their homes yet to me, they were the evil ones who were partially responsible for where I was in my life. I suppose I sound like the victim and even though I felt I was, I had to get my mind off that and start concentrating on being the winner in all this if I was to survive.

There were times I just felt like throwing in the towel. I didn't want to be here anymore but then something would kick in and I would tell myself that I would win in the end.

It is true what they say when you keep looking back it stops you from moving forward. I had to start getting rid of the past and stop being the victim.

Life had not been kind, but in saying that, I had many opportunities that could have worked but I was always looking for something else. I was never satisfied with what

I had when I had it but isn't that what we are taught? To look at the bigger picture and go for it. I had never been a risk taker, and I looked at others who had made it but I suppose we don't see what goes on under the surface. It always looked so easy.

I had been stripped of my confidence ever since I had given up the job I loved at the newspaper to become a Councillor in local government. A poor paying position to try and help my community. A thankless, tireless job that was not worth all the heartache and pain.

It was obvious by now I had always chosen the wrong path for my life; I had to start making the right choices and get my confidence back. But how?

It was always my belief that families were there through thick and thin to support each other in times of need but not in my case. I was angry all the time yet knew that what I was feeling was not going to get me anywhere. I was alone and that was how it was, I had to accept it. There was no knight in shining armour to help me. Nor was there going to be.

I still questioned why my past relationships that infected my life to begin with were doing so well. Bryce and Brad seemed to have it all. I couldn't understand why I was the one who had to go through what I called hell.

They had their relationships and their homes yet to me, they were the evil ones who were partially responsible for where I was in my life. I suppose I sound like the victim and even though I felt I was, I had to get my mind off that and start concentrating on being the winner in all this if I was to survive.

There were times I just felt like throwing in the towel. I didn't want to be here anymore but then something would kick in and I would tell myself that I would win in the end.

It is true what they say when you keep looking back it stops you from moving forward. I had to start getting rid of the past and stop being the victim.

Life had not been kind, but in saying that, I had many opportunities that could have worked but I was always looking for something else. I was never satisfied with what

I had when I had it but isn't that what we are taught? To look at the bigger picture and go for it. I had never been a risk taker, and I looked at others who had made it but I suppose we don't see what goes on under the surface. It always looked so easy.

I had been stripped of my confidence ever since I had given up the job I loved at the newspaper to become a Councillor in local government. A poor paying position to try and help my community. A thankless, tireless job that was not worth all the heartache and pain.

It was obvious by now I had always chosen the wrong path for my life; I had to start making the right choices and get my confidence back. But how?

Chapter 10

WHO AM I?

I started to wonder who I really was. A woman, a mother, an employer. So many depended on me. I had to start gaining the confidence for my business to survive, and I knew that much about me. I was and am a survivor. My responsibility was to myself first, and then to others. That's where I went wrong. Always putting others before myself. I was known as the rescuer.

Now, it was time to take the bull by the horns and get to where I wanted to be, and that was a successful woman in my own right. After all, I had been too busy looking after everyone else to think about myself.

It was spring, the better weather was coming and I had every reason to believe my business would improve. There were a few interested buyers but no one had put an offer in, and I kept wondering if this was another lesson I had to learn. Do I have to get through this to get to the other side? Was that what the universe was trying to tell me? Hard work, don't look back, just keep going – that was how I would achieve my goal.

Bills were piling up and I had to make the money last. I was living on an oily rag and knew suppliers would start pounding on the door at any moment. It is an awful feeling to owe people money but I had to keep the business afloat. I always depended on the weekends to bring at least the wages in so I could pay those that worked for me.

The rent was overdue again and I knew the landlord would be paying me a visit, I would say to myself just stretch it out. It was always due on the 1st of the month; I tried to buy an extra couple of weeks as I knew September would be a better month with the school holidays just two weeks away.

Little by little, I would have to make it work, so I started giving suppliers just a little every week. Someone would have to wait. Just how long I could go on like this was beyond me.

Weekends, you would think, would get better. As I said, that was my bread and butter but the first week in September was not looking good. Not even many for Father's Day. I didn't understand.

I had come to realise it was not the community who was going to push me forward and out of the red to the black, it was the holidaymakers and there were few of those coming to town.

No matter how often I told myself it was all going to change, everything was becoming such a strain. My mum told me on a daily basis not to worry, to just keep going, it will change. She had so much faith but it was so difficult, and I felt my health was getting worse. Smoking again was having a bad effect on me but I didn't care at the time. I was lonely and confused and just felt like throwing in the towel.

I know it sounds like I felt sorry for myself and the truth is, I did. My family was dysfunctional and I was lonely and tired with no one to help me out of the mess I found myself in. None of my children would come and lend a hand.

The nights and the days just dragged on and the loneliness was unbearable. I couldn't even cry; I had no energy, just kept feeling the despair to the point I didn't want to be here anymore. Even found myself thinking how nice it would be just to go to sleep and never wake up again. I knew that was wrong but I was in such an emotional state at the time.

I used to ask myself repeatedly, *why?* I had done all the right things – marketing, had great food and a nice restaurant with a lovely atmosphere. It really was nothing I was doing wrong. It came down to location. I could scream now, looking back, that I was stupid getting myself into that situation in the first place. At that time, I had a real problem making the right choices for my life, and I just needed to turn it around. Quite frankly, I felt it was in the lap of the gods. Had I bought in spring and not winter it all would have worked out perfectly. But I didn't. The money I would make in the summer would get me through the next winter and that's what everyone did who had a business in a holiday destination. I had done it all back to front and, as an elderly gentleman told me, he had seen so many restaurants close because there was no support from the locals, they just didn't go out.

My children were constantly on my mind although I knew my youngest boys were always there for me and truly loved me. The eldest of my younger two boys was living in Brisbane to try and get closer to his dad; this was the boy that ran after his dad's car when he was four, when Bryce left him the first time. He was still insecure and just wanted a relationship with Bryce, which was never to be. He thought he could live with Bryce but that was not to be either. He had to share a home with his wife's younger sister and that was not what he wanted. As I said, my son wanted to rebuild his life with his father and thought he would be welcome to stay in his home even if it was just until he got on his feet.

The youngest was always so busy with school and his football at the time but still both boys always called to see if I was okay. Even on Father's Day they both texted me to say happy Father's Day. They said I deserved that because I was not only their mother but their dad as well.

My eldest son and daughter were oblivious to my feelings and didn't have the same compassion that my younger boys had. It's funny that they were all from the same family, different dads and so totally disparate. I just had to accept that the eldest really didn't care for me anymore. By this time, my daughter had sided with my eldest son and she didn't have much time for me either. They were selfish. Only worried about themselves. They didn't take after me but were very much like their father, whereas the younger ones had more compassion even though they didn't come and help me in the restaurant. They had that compassion for others which is a quality that is so important in life, and they didn't judge me for the mistakes I had made.

It is true that we are all born with our own personality, although at the end of the day I still believed loving families should support each other through thick and thin.

I had been in the townhouse I lived in for over 12 months and my eldest daughter and eldest son had not even given me the time of day. Not even a phone call just to say hi and to see if I was still living. It was apparent that no one cared, which just made me feel worse and a failure as a parent.

Sorry, there I go again. Woe is me, playing the victim. I really had to move on and get out of this terrible state of mind. Time to start looking at the positives, for the things I needed to be grateful.

I don't know where I would have been without my girlfriend Andrea, who lived in Brisbane. She called me every day of every year, always supportive, just like my mum. I realised if I didn't have them, God knows where I would be in this lonely shell I had found myself in. So, at least I wasn't alone. From time to time, I had found myself thinking about all the lonely people in the world that no one gives a thought about.

I thought a lot about the elderly over that time, and how a lot of families desert them when they are placed in homes. When I was about 10 years old, I was with the Red Cross, and we would visit them in the homes for the elderly. I would make them fans out of icy poles sticks and remembered how happy they were just having someone to talk with. It always made me happy that I was making others feel good, which is where I started always being the giver. That's who I became right through my life.

It's not wrong to give, what I am saying is that giving too much of yourself can be a mistake because so many can end up taking you for granted.

Although I knew I had to push myself to become more positive about my situation, it was hard. Still, I was determined that I had to change the way I was thinking. I had to block out all the bad and start living like the book, *The Secret*, tells us to.

For those who don't know, *The Secret*, is a self-help book written by Rhonda Byrne. The book is very enlightening and details the way we can attract a better life. I decided every morning I would get out of bed and look at life differently. At night, I would visualise what I wanted when I went to bed. I wanted so much for someone to buy the restaurant so I could move on before it killed me.

Chapter 11

STAYING POSITIVE

How does anyone stay positive in bad situations like this? I suppose I had no choice, otherwise the inevitable would happen. I had to discipline my mind because it is all about our thoughts. Remember, what we think about we bring about.

It is not an easy task staying positive when you are looking at your bank account and you know time and money is running out, but you have to. The broker had made an appointment with me on a Monday to show some people through the restaurant – they were locals, so I felt that was a positive sign as they would know the area well. They knew that spring was the right time to buy. The restaurant was going to be so busy over the summer months, which, as I said, would set them up and carry them through the next winter. I could not survive; I didn't have enough money to get to the summer and my health was getting worse, I had to sell.

The appointment was for 5.30pm, and I was so nervous – they had to be the buyers. I kept saying, "let this nightmare be over." Surely, it must be my turn to have a break so life can be normal again. I deserve to win this time. Deserve to have a better life, and I certainly deserve to be happy.

I would visualise the restaurant selling and a sold sign right across the front window.

The appointment went well and there was another buyer interested, so I knew it was going to sell. I had called the previous owner to see if he wanted to buy it back, much cheaper than I had paid him for it. He didn't; however, he passed on my details to someone he thought may be interested. The previous owner was a complete bastard but he did get the wheels in motion, so to speak.

In the meantime, I took some chill-out time, a lunch with my favourite friends talking about the past few years and the behind-closed-doors stuff one does not talk about. I had not mentioned earlier in the book but there were moments I did certain things I was not proud of yet did not regret, purely because I was lonely.

I reminisced with my girlfriends about my one-night stand in Sydney, it was one of those times Brad had dropped me. Never would I have thought I would have done such a thing but guess what? I did, and for some reason it was not only good but right for me. I can't tell you who he was because I don't remember his name. It was too long ago but I do remember he was good looking and intelligent. Too much to hope for in today's world, I suppose.

He was a nice person; I got lucky. We met in a bar, and

I was very lonely. I think he was too. Never had I done that before, never even contemplated I ever would but I did, and I have no regrets. I will never forget that evening with him. He was a gentleman and made me feel like a woman should. The man was only 40 and a good lover – exactly what the doctor ordered. I never saw him again. It was just one night I would remember forever.

I wasn't going to bash myself up over it; what happens in our private life should not be anyone else's business, and I don't think anyone should sit in judgment... do you?

Life had not been kind to me, so it was nice to spend an evening with a stranger.

Back to my hopeful selling. The guy who knew the previous owner called to enquire about the restaurant. He already owned another in the next town and was very successful. He now wanted to buy another business. I hadn't heard from the first buyers, so I accepted his offer even though it was $25,000 under the asking price. At that stage, I didn't care, I just wanted out. The landlord was being an absolute horror to me and hassling me about the previous tenant who had not fixed certain items when he left it to me. I was not about to take on that responsibility. It was all getting so hard for this sale to go through, as I had just discovered I didn't have the lease transferred to me when I had bought.

What a nightmare I had found myself in. I ended up telling the landlord if he didn't let this sale go through, then we would both lose, so it was in his best interest to let me out of the lease.

I couldn't wait, although I was scared of what I was going to do to make money. Even not knowing what the future would hold for me, I kept on moving forward. All I knew was that I wanted to be out of the town I had come to hate.

Despite the beautiful landscape, it was a miserable place and it truly was a huge mistake on my part.

I just kept thinking, *just another man who has ripped me off.* It's true. These last six years I had allowed so many men to completely rip me off one way or another. Let them all get away with it. Not only that, I had lived through the worst 26 weeks of my life. In saying that, I had also learned so much that would be invaluable to me in the future.

My family was a complete disappointment; not one of my children were there to help me. That alone was enough to make me wonder what happened to the meaning of family.

When the chips were down, you should be able to depend on those closest to you. Not in my case. It was just another lesson. One I will take to my grave. I had given so much to my family my whole life. My main purpose revolved around making sure my children had everything they needed yet here I was, alone and in trouble. There was no one on whom I could depend.

The rent was still overdue and I had so many bills, I was just hoping the buyer would sign any day and I could start moving forward. Still, I had no word from him. I was worried.

I can't remember another time in my life I felt so helpless, but I had to keep focused, couldn't allow it to get the better of me.

Throughout my life, I had really tried to be a good person. It was so unfair this was happening to me.

In the meantime, I would lay in bed applying for jobs till it was time to go to work. It was so frustrating. Someone, somewhere, had to give me a break. I had to keep faith that it was all going to work out and, with the exception of my family, it would all come together. I had grown up with a lot of faith and I felt this was a real test. I had to stay strong.

One thing I will say is, I didn't feel like a failure. I knew I had tried, and that's all that mattered. Although, my eldest son felt differently. He had sent me the worst email I have ever received, telling me I was a fake and he knew I couldn't do anything, which I read to mean he thought I was a huge failure. He thought so little of me. That was depressing in and of itself, and I will never forget that.

At last the contracts were signed and I had a settlement date 27th October, 2010. I was so relieved. Bills were still piling up, so I faxed all the suppliers telling them the restaurant was sold and they would be paid on the 28th

October, which would buy me some time. It was important that I walked away clean and owed no one anything.

It was incredible timing when my chef gave a week's notice on the 6th of October and I signed the contract on the 7th. I knew I had no choice but to close on the 10th. What else could I do? I had no chef and my contract stated I had to stay open until the 17th.

I rang the buyer and asked him if I could leave a week earlier as I had given him permission to move in on the 18th despite settlement being the 27th. He agreed, as he would be renovating. I had to close that deal giving him $1000 worth of stock. He was an astute businessman who really didn't care about my situation. He called it 'loss of goodwill'; a bit ridiculous, really, when you think about it. More a way of getting a bit more out of me. He was closing anyway to renovate, so what was another week to him?

A selfish man who couldn't care about anyone but himself. I couldn't understand how anyone could be so cold.

The last day felt like such a relief. I really didn't have many staff by this stage and we all left on a lovely note. No regrets. In fact, I felt so grateful that I was out of it as I had learned so many lessons in such a short time. The value of money, family, and about who I was.

The business had a bad effect on my health, and now I had to concentrate on my future and rebuild my life for the final time.

Chapter 12

MY NEW LIFE

I had put in so many applications for positions but no one ever replied which, once again, felt like it did the previous year but this time it was different. I had lost over $128,000 in just 26 weeks, and now had to find a job to rebuild my life and save for my home.

I didn't really want to go back to real estate but I saw a job advertised and the principal's name was John. When I saw his picture, I realised I had worked with him in 1992 when Bryce had left me the first time when my boys were toddlers.

He had worked for me back then as a property manager and when he left, he went into sales and bought his own business in another suburb. He was a lovely family Italian guy and I knew this could be the way to rebuild my life and get myself into a better financial position.

The office was within 15 minutes of my home where Brad lived – the man I went out with who ripped me off financially and emotionally. Brad left me for another woman 15 years his junior. I didn't want to go back there but I couldn't let that stand in my way; I had to start a new life.

John hired me on the spot and I was starting on the 20th of October, seven days before my settlement. It wasn't my dream job. I would have much preferred to have secured a position in local government as an employee, but it was not on the cards for me. Maybe this was where I would get myself back on track and make some money to start again.

I have to tell you it was so scary to be in the position I found myself in. Going into a job I was not fond of but knowing if I did it right, it could set me up for the rest of my life.

There was no doubt in my mind that I would make it. I am a survivor, and nothing would stand in my way this time.

I had a friend who was 101 years old, that's right, 101. She was a beautiful woman; her name was Doreen and an inspiration to me. It's funny how you don't know a whole lot about someone's life until the day of their funeral. She was amazing; her husband walked out on her when she was a young woman with two small boys and she worked three jobs to survive. Her story really inspired me. To this day, I carry her picture in my work diary to remind me that anything is possible. I hope she knows how important she was to me, an inspiration!

Just imagine in those days being in that position and although we had never spoken about her past, I knew she was an amazing woman. She gave me so much courage and she probably never even knew. It was funny because her son had told me before she passed away that she had said she wanted to go into real estate with me. She didn't know at that time that it was a plan of mine, so maybe she knew something I didn't. Doreen celebrated her 101st birthday in my restaurant, and I was so honoured to have her there. I will never forget her. She was and is my mentor, someone I aspire to be.

I had a run in with Bryce about our eldest son because he had disowned him, and I will never understand how a parent can do that. Bryce left him running after his car in 1992 saying, "Daddy come back", when he was just four years old. So, it came as no surprise that he was still sending the same painful message to our son.

My son was now 21, and his father thought so little of him. He had no direction in life, no future in anything. It had all started because our son had been living in Brisbane for three months wanting so bad to get close to his dad but realised his dad wasn't the man he thought he was. My son grew lonelier and lonelier in Brisbane and decided he needed to come home. He had no family there. Bryce was always too busy with his new wife and his own life, and had even sent our son a text message saying he should think of him as dead now. How could any parent say that to their child? One should never ever give up on their children, that is my belief. There is hope for everyone.

I often wonder if the world would be different if all the parents took responsibility for those they bring into the world. Bryce had to realise that no one is perfect. We all make mistakes, and that was no different for his son. Maybe time spent with him would have made the world of difference. I remember after Bryce left in 1992, our son was so traumatised my eldest sister's husband, his uncle, spent time with him. It was so comforting to this little boy who felt deserted. They walked on the beach and had fun, and to this day, he has never forgotten how special those moments were with his godfather.

Chapter 13

OCTOBER 16TH – MEMORIES

My son was back home and I was relieved in a way as he was sitting for his police entrance exam on the 6th anniversary since his father had walked out. I prayed and prayed that morning he would pass, he just had to. He needed so much to create a future for himself, and he was low on confidence by this stage. He had a car accident the day before and things were not going right. I thought, it had been six years and surely things should be changing for the better; we had suffered enough and yet Bryce was living a lovely life.

How could that be? All I ever wanted was for my boys to be really happy and have a great life. Isn't that what most parents want for their children?

I remember thinking back to that Saturday morning when our lives changed forever. I thought I had actually moved forward but I still held much resentment.

There was nothing I wanted more than for both my sons to be okay, to have their careers – one in the police force and one a teacher. Then I would be able to get on with my own life. At this point, I realised I had been raising children for 39 years and still had not had my own life. I think most of you would agree there is something wrong with that picture, and I had not really enjoyed my life up to that point. During all that time, I had to be the breadwinner, the mum, the dad and make all things right even though the boys were old enough to stand on their own two feet. Still, as a parent, I felt I had not taught them to be accountable for their own lives.

I had to change the memory of this day. My son sitting his exam and me looking at yet another rental, only this time in a beautiful place called Sandhurst. However, after investigating the rental market, I realised it was not going to work for me – the market was so high.

The boys and I needed a change and we had to make a new beginning after the restaurant mess. This time, I had to make everything work for all of us. My son would not find out for two weeks whether he passed his exam so in the meantime, I had to keep moving forward even though it was the 16th and that day was filled with bad memories.

It had to be a new beginning.

I couldn't help but remember our beautiful home we had built and how I wished I was still there. It would have made such a difference if Bryce and I could have raised our boys together. Their lives would not be in such turmoil and they would not have gone through all the upheavals I put them through.

Guilt gnawed at me, my belief I was an unstable parent,

although I still believed I had done the best I could for them. We did live in some lovely homes and I should have realised when I had bought my first home after Bryce left that it would have been the best decision to stay there because I would not be putting us all through the upheaval again.

In hindsight, I should have, could have. There I go again, looking back all the time. This behaviour had to stop, and I had to start looking only forward. I had to wake up every morning with a new dream, one that would make us all happy.

I did feel my life was moving forward finally. Even though the debts were piling up, I knew I would come out okay. That is what having faith is all about. I was about to start my new job and I kept telling myself I would be successful.

Through my whole experience in the restaurant, I had learned so many lessons and was about to embark on a new journey that I would make my life.

The new owner of the restaurant was making it difficult for me by making me spend more money because of some maintenance issues he felt were my responsibility. They weren't. He had already taken an extra $6000 off me. Then the landlord's lawyer put his own price on just surrendering my lease. What more did I have to go through to put this mess behind me? How much did I have to lose to move forward? The fees from the landlord's lawyer were ridiculous to say the least, but I had no option. I had to pay whatever they asked. It was thousands.

I had to accept all the conditions they were putting on me as I was in a vulnerable position. It was costing me a fortune and there was nothing I could do but pay them. It was just another man ripping me off; it had become the story of my life. There was no question the landlord's lawyer had me over a barrel.

It was so unfair, but what could I do? My financial position was in their hands if I was to get out of it with something. I had to comply with the health department and fix everything, even though none of this had been done by the previous tenant. I was on the home run, just two weeks to go and it would all be over.

Could it get any worse? At this stage, I wasn't sure. It was all such a nightmare. My eldest son, who wanted to be the chef and disowned me, had sent me awful text messages; the 'F' word used frequently, saying he hated me and wanted nothing to do with me. He was obviously having financial problems, which he would not accept was his own doing. No one forced his wife to leave her job to go into the restaurant. It was her decision, and not my responsibility. We are all accountable for our own decisions in life. He had put no money into the restaurant, so I couldn't understand why he was blaming me.

I just wanted life to move on to a better place. It was

hard knowing I had lost my eldest son and his family forever; they accepted no blame in the whole restaurant fiasco. If only we could have all acknowledged our part in it, we would have been fine. I loved all of my children—warts and all—that was a given but they didn't see the problems they caused for me. I felt sorry that my grandchildren had to go through the entire trauma. All I wanted was for everyone to be happy and my family to be that perfect picture.

Why, oh why did this have to happen?

Why can't things change? Yes, I suppose I was feeling sorry for myself but understandably so at this stage.

The same old saying always came to mind: If it's going to be, it's up to me.

Now, the time had come for me to go back into real estate. I had to make it work. To never look back, and only be grateful for the opportunity. Nothing could be as hard as the restaurant.

When I took the job with John, I didn't realise he only had two listings; however, it was a nice office to work in and we all got along very well. I would go out walking, dropping pamphlets every morning in the hope that we would get some response. John was a lovely man and very genuine. He was going through his own issues with a marriage breakup and he was not in a good financial position, although he was growing his property management which kept his business afloat. That was not going to help me. I realised one day at the front desk I could nearly see Brad's house from where I was sitting at reception, and I was so worried about running into him, which I avoided at all costs. It made me wonder why I ended up back near Brad. It was just full of bad memories for me but it was a lovely place and everyone was friendly.

Even though I had found a position in real estate, I was still in an awful mindset with my eldest children not talking to me. The only thing on my mind was setting a good example for my two youngest boys. I just had to give them some family as they also were cut from their eldest brother's life. None of it was fair or of their doing.

Luke was and is a beautiful person of whom I was proud. He was my youngest and reminded me so much of my daughter; so self-sufficient. They were switched on and looked for opportunity, not like my first child, Jack, who thought the world owed him something.

My life now was in turmoil, waiting for the closure of the restaurant and ending up with very little money. I was so over it and just wanted it all to end. At times, I really didn't want to be here anymore and in the back of my mind were my two ex-husbands saying I would end up alone... and here I was.

Where to now? I asked myself every day. Why couldn't I get a job that I really wanted and have that feeling every morning to jump out of bed and be excited about my day? It wasn't a lot to ask. I remember feeling like that when I was at the newspaper, and I so very much wanted that feeling again.

I felt isolated, and I had no one except for my mum who had been so supportive through everything – an 82-year-old woman who had taught me to be so courageous and had such high principles.

My daughter had sent me an email saying I had only myself to blame, and I made my life what it is. I suppose that was true. There were many mistakes I had made, but I was the only one who had to live with the consequences, the only one who had to try and change it. We all make mistakes and I never believed in putting others down because of their choices, be they right or wrong. I wasn't a fabulous grandparent, for which my eldest children resented me, constantly reminded me of it but I still loved my grandchildren, regardless of what they thought.

I was a parent at 17, and for 39 years had been raising kids. If that is seen as selfish to anyone, then so be it. I never felt that way, and had not experienced my own life up to that point. Even Bryce was off the hook. He was only a father for 14 years, so I really felt I was a little entitled to think of myself and my own life at the age of 57.

As I mentioned earlier, what gives anyone the right to criticize others until they walk in the same shoes, until they know how it feels? Our lives are all so different and each and every person handles emotions their own way, just as I did. I felt the stirrings of depression. No real family and a job I didn't really want but was grateful to have something. I just had to keep pushing myself but my loneliness was getting the better of me.

I had paid out all the suppliers of the restaurant—around $28,000—which was depressing to say the least. What was worse was coming home to an empty house every night and staring at the four walls.

As I said, I was really lonely and had no one at this point in my life.

Going to work turned out not to be that bad after all. I had an opportunity I had to make happen if I were ever to get past the way I was feeling. It didn't help still being a mother and hoping one day my youngest boys would find their lives.

This last week had been the worst for me, and if it had not have been for my boys, I wouldn't be here. They needed me however I felt. I had to stay focused and strong.

My mum was great but she is just one person; I needed my children but they were far from supportive in my time of need.

My eldest son and his wife were never coming back into my life; I knew that. My eldest son had become someone I didn't know anymore and his wife was not the person I thought she was. She was bitter and twisted.

Life was not being fair, through my eyes. I just had to keep going and knew if I worked hard and stayed focused,

I could make it. It was just getting used to the lonely life after hours.

I will never understand unsupportive families. Love is supposed to be unconditional. Nobody should ever be put down for making mistakes.

Chapter 14

THE PENNY DROPPED – THE MIND SHIFT

Going to work was hard enough, especially to a job I thought I hated. Then one morning after speaking to my girlfriend Andrea, I was starting to realise there was some connection between my continuous moves with jobs and homes. I had moved 31 times in my life since I was just 17 years of age. There was something wrong with that. I had been so restless since Bryce had left six years prior, and I had lost so much financially and personally, so I started to evaluate what that could mean.

There had always been restlessness, no matter where I lived or who I worked for, that nothing would be right in my life if I didn't change. Stability was what I needed. To stick to something and start enjoying my life. Be more confident with where I was right now in my life. It wasn't about the job or where I lived, it was all about me and my confusion with life itself and everything I had been through. Quite frankly, it's a wonder I have survived the last six years of turmoil.

It was time to change. To get rid of my addictions and mean it. Wake up happy every day and look forward to going to work. That was at least a start. Remember, misery brings more misery and I was well and truly over that feeling. I could be whoever I wanted to be, and there was nothing that was going to stop me.

My boss, John, had said to me if I worked hard there was no reason why I couldn't buy another home within the next two years. I held onto those words because I desperately wanted my own home again, to be financially independent. If I applied myself, I could make it happen.

I had been given another opportunity, and this time it had to be different.

It was then I picked up *The Law of Attraction* again, promising myself that I would only attract good things into my life.

My picture-perfect family was never to be a reality. I had to accept it. What choice did I have?

Today would be a new beginning – one of hope for the future, one with no regrets. If I have learned anything through my journey, it is to never give up on yourself, to just fill your mind with only positive thoughts. Shut all the people out around you that make you feel bad and surround yourself with optimistic people who enjoy your company.

I am now starting to see where my future will be, and I just know my boys will be okay. They have their own journey and I am sure that I have now turned the corner, they will be far better off for it.

One thing we all realise in life is that it is not what happens to us but how we handle it, how to bring about positive change.

I made a promise to myself to look at everything in life differently, to rise above anything or anyone that gets in my way. I love the way I feel today. It is a feeling of such optimism and just knowing life can be whatever I choose it to be and *not* because of what happens to me. It has taken me six years to get to this point but I am finally here and that is all that matters. Success is not that far away. All I had to do is reach out and touch it, make it happen.

There was still the desire to move to another home; I was tired of living in a townhouse and knew that it would be much better for me and the boys. I had left my home on the water because of Brad, not because I didn't like it. It was because he was living so close to me. I was not afraid of that feeling anymore, and was entitled to live wherever I chose.

Since working with John, I had gotten to know some of the people in the community and it was starting to feel like home.

Life with the boys, though, was becoming increasingly difficult. Particularly the eldest of the two. He always thought someone owed him a living instead of getting up and making it happen for himself. I find it hard to refuse giving him money when he needs it but I know I have to stop. There is no other way to make him understand that we are all accountable; however, I am fully aware I created this burden, giving him so much over the years. I swear he thinks I am a money tree that will never run out.

He is not aware that it *is* running out, and we all have to pull our weight if we are to survive financially. I am confident I will get back on my feet, but he needs to learn about money. It is frightening that he doesn't understand that at the age of nearly 22.

Both boys had the same upbringing and yet they both handled it differently.

Young men need to understand the importance of responsibility at a young age and I don't blame him entirely. The blame lies with me as the parent, both as mother and father. I obviously didn't get it right. These are the times I start to feel extraordinarily resentful towards Bryce because he is *also* responsible. This is his son I am talking about. Bryce is free and living a wonderful life with his wife, and obviously carries no guilt about our boys. To me, that was and is wrong. As a parent, I could not be so irresponsible. What was the point in having children? Why have them and say you want them only to end up leaving them? What if I had chosen to turn my back on them? What would have become of them? I shudder to think.

My life had been a rollercoaster over the past six years, and now it was time to get it together and be happy. I am still having a hard time with my family. They are dysfunctional, and there is no end in sight. Still to this day, I cannot see my eldest son and his family ever coming back to me but that is out of my control. I can't do anything about that and quite frankly they have treated me so badly. I should have told them that should they wish to be a part of this family then they needed to get over it.

Families should be able to say what they think and move on. Not act like children and have that childish hatred that is so unbecoming in anyone. It's called maturity, and sometimes it takes some of our children much longer to grow up, but then sometimes, it can be all too late.

Life is still a lonely place but I somehow get the feeling that in time, it will change. I think the last emails from my eldest son closed the door forever; they were so hurtful and unnecessary. How much should any mother endure? The jealousy he felt for his brothers was so unbelievably sad.

These are his words, verbatim.

'You really are warped, maybe all the alcohol has soaked up the remaining cells you have left... we bought the boys gifts you ignorant bitch every year, but whatever, and as for money why don't you get that son of yours to pay up on all the handouts he got, and as for my grandmother she can have you all as the last few times I have spoken to her all I coped was abuse about you and how I have done this, well you can all get fucked I never want to see any of your clan again...I don't blame my father or Bryce for their actions and now have no issues with Bryce as I can only imagine what it must have been like living with you. You only have to look at your life and look at your loneliness to realise who you truly are, ask yourself and be honest for the first time in your life, you are full of faults but claim to be the victim in every case and constantly burn people...your one true friend is in Queensland! Wow, do the math...distance relationships work for you as no one can stand being around you. As far as I am concerned I have divorced myself from you and want no further contact from any of you can't make it any clearer. STAY AWAY ALL OF YOU !!!!!!!!!!!!! I can live with that and am comfortable with the same. *Your ex-son.*'

And then there was this email (verbatim) on the same day! As I said, how much should a mother endure after all the sacrifices one makes for her children?

'My God you are truly delusional, the boys, the boys, the boys, that's all we hear, well fuck them, they are only half brothers at best who never bother with anyone but their own needs, isn't it funny how my life has to revolve around them every event, every birthday, every Christmas and if I didn't bother, well the wrath I would receive wasn't worth it...you, on occasions, do have a good heart yet that comes with conditions...you have taken from me more than you have ever possibly given...

remember my wedding when I had no choice but to have Bryce as my best man because as you say, family will always be there...remember my graduation when I wasn't allowed to spend time with my father...oh my God I could go on but can't be assed...fuck the lot of you hope to never see you all ever again, you can have your perfect sons. *See ya.*'

Can anyone believe that a son could be so hostile and cruel? I have to live everyday knowing I gave up my whole life just to have him at the age of 17. Now, I ask myself, why? I had to put all of this out of my mind, his family no longer existed.

Every day that passed was going to get better and I was committed to making my dreams come true. That's all that mattered at the time. I was not going to let my eldest son's hostility get in my way.

The next afternoon, he dumped all my paperwork from the restaurant on my back veranda. It was all stored at his home because his wife was keeping the books, and even though we didn't speak, I kept her employed, so we would email for business purposes. He not only dropped paperwork, but dumped rubbish such as large flags and other items that were unnecessary and no use to me. After his awful emails and dumping all that rubbish, I decided enough was enough and he would be out of my thoughts forever.

I had to let go of this insanity once and for all.

By this stage, I was feeling quite happy at work and had settled in but I had gone to see a financial advisor at the bank after I repaid the loan and the extra money I had borrowed for the restaurant. My savings were getting lower and I knew I had to change something to survive. She was great to talk to but said I needed a job that paid me a better wage.

She explained that if I didn't sell enough property with the real estate company I worked for on a regular basis, I would run out of money very quickly. I really wasn't making enough to cover my weekly expenses, so this time I had to think long and hard about what I was going to do. On one hand, others in real estate did well, why shouldn't I? But that had not been happening for me, and I had not even one listing despite it only being three weeks since I had started. I had to be patient to reap the rewards; after all, Rome wasn't built in a day.

Every now and again, Bryce and Brad both would creep into my mind. The resentment towards them remained, although the money situation was my own responsibility. I had made so many financial mistakes through my emotional state over the past six years, and it was my entire fault. There was no one else to blame. I should have been in control, although it is not uncommon for anyone to make mistakes when forming decisions whilst under so much stress.

It happens to so many people.

If I had of gone to a financial advisor years prior, I would not have found myself in this position. In fact, I would have lived comfortably. At my age, I should have been looking at living a comfortable life, and I couldn't help but have regrets. How on Earth was I going to pull myself out of it?

I needed to get healthy. Stop smoking and lose weight. That was the beginning to getting my life back. We all know how great it feels when we shed those unwanted kilos and start to look at ourselves differently. A lovely young girl named Kristee who I worked with in the office decided we were both going to tackle this problem together. We both wanted to lose weight, so we made a promise that we would encourage each other to achieve our goals. I felt so good, even after a couple of days. I knew I was on the right track and just started looking at food as the enemy. Besides, I was still a young woman myself, even at the age of 57. I knew in my heart more happiness was to come if I became disciplined in everything I did. At least, that was my dream. I knew it was all achievable, and after everything I had been through, knew more than anything I deserved to be happy.

Chapter 15

THEY ARE JUST FEELINGS

I was walking out of my office, and lo and behold there was Brad in the café next door. I was horrified at first but was looking at the back of him. It suddenly dawned on me. What did I ever see in him? He was such a slob. Brad still looked the same, in the familiar baggy, old shorts with his stomach protruding out under his t-shirt, and barefoot, of course. I must have been insane to go out with him. He didn't even care about his appearance.

Previously, I was so frightened of running into him but it was the best thing that could have happened because it made me realise those feelings I had been carrying with me—the hurt and the pain—were just that, feelings. They didn't exist. I really didn't feel any emotion at all for him, and just kept walking as if I had not noticed.

He was someone I wished I had never been involved with in the first place. It is good to confront one's emotions because they really are just a memory. We hang on to them for so long without realising that letting them go will give us a much happier life without that person in it.

I have come to the realisation whilst writing *Escaping a Narcissistic Marriage* that I had been very driven by feelings and emotions, which is something most of us don't realise. Whether we are in a relationship for three months or three years, we take those emotions with us into the next relationship, which is where it all goes wrong. Since I have stopped smoking and drinking, it feels like a dark cloud has lifted from my head. All of a sudden I can see what has happened to me and everyone around me. It truly is an amazing experience to be able to recognise how all this is possible.

You realise that a crazy moment seemed to last forever, but it is actually about not wanting to be alone. It's more about being insecure with yourself. Once you can feel comfortable with who you are, then all the negative starts to unravel.

The realisation is that we are all alone, one way or another. I spend so much time by myself it mostly doesn't seem to bother me... maybe a little some nights, but generally I have become accustomed to that feeling of isolation. I am not saying I wouldn't like to meet someone because I would. All I am saying is that it doesn't hurt anymore. Once you get used to your own company, you have no choice. Sometimes, that's just the way life is.

I do, however, sway back and forwards in my thoughts sometimes. It is unbearable but then I have to remind myself I am okay.

One thing I am very much looking forward to is moving house. I am hoping it is soon because the place I am living in is depressing in itself. I need a change. Need to move onto the next chapter of my life.

Working in real estate has been difficult so say the least. Trying to get new listings was particularly hard since I had found out the other local agents were putting us down to potential clients. I had to figure a way around it because I had made up my mind I was going to be a success.

I put in an application for a property in Sandhurst, which is where I believed it would be best for me and the boys. Originally, it was a little expensive but I had to pay a little more than I thought because I just couldn't get anything else. Even if I had to get a second job on my only day off, I thought it would be worth it. Now, I had to be patient, something at which I really was not good. Waiting was always hard for me because I always seemed to be waiting for something great to come into my life. My mother was so right when she said patience is a virtue!

Within a month of working for John, I got my first listing and had two others on the go. I told myself everyday it was a sign of good things to come. My boys seemed to be going backwards, in particular the eldest. He had come back from Brisbane; had been drinking, and I couldn't cope with the way things were. It had to change.

Loneliness crept into my life once again. It was something I had never gotten used to. I was not one of those people who could go and sit in a bar or go to a nightclub on my own, it just wasn't me. Time passes, and I had been doing so well with not smoking and drinking. I was feeling so much better losing weight as well, and wanted the old me to return – the one I loved that could look in the mirror and be full of confidence. I was a believer that life had something great in store for me. It had to. I just had to keep faith.

I don't know what it is about young people today, they don't seem to have that inner strength that makes them strive for the best in life. Certainly, there are some that have it but the majority I see, just don't. They think life owes them something, and I had to find a way to change that in my boys, but I had no idea how.

My initial thought was to have them pay something towards our living expenses because they continued to think I would look after them forever.

It's funny, but my youngest son said to me that his dad didn't have much money so he couldn't go to him although Bryce had two homes and a great life living the executive couple with no kids. I don't know what he thought I had when I didn't even have my own home or why he saw me as a money tree when he knew my circumstances. It didn't make any sense to me with the way either of them thought. They watched me work six days a week and couldn't even make their beds or help with the housework. I felt so bad because it had to be my fault; I was the one that raised them.

They should have been taught how to cook and be self-sufficient, otherwise how could they live with anyone in the future? My immediate thoughts were of the poor girls they would end up with; they will just take over from where I left off. I can't help but feel responsible for the way they have turned out. Don't get me wrong, they were compassionate human beings but very lazy. Just like most teenagers, I suppose.

I had been so tied up in my emotions over the last crucial six years of their life when I should have been present and mindful of what I should have taught them. This bashing myself up over the 'what ifs' had to stop. It was now or never. Although, I will admit that the most important things I had taught them had sunk in – love and compassion.

The property to rent in Sandhurst fell through. There were four applicants, and one offered more rent than everyone else, which I thought was not right but it obviously wasn't meant to be so I continued looking for the right property. My boys did not want to leave the only town they knew, the only home they had known. It was convenient for them. Their friends were there and they had already moved so many times that they didn't want to move again.

My youngest was waiting to hear from university and he really deserved to get in. Again, there was that word 'patience'. It was difficult waiting all the time for anything good to happen. He had just finished his diploma after two years and he had worked hard in that time, I was proud of him.

He wanted to be a PE teacher and had dreams of becoming an AFL coach. Although he didn't come out and say it, I knew what direction he was heading. He had already coached an under-12s footy team for a local club for a season and now was moving on to coach another football team. This time, under-15s.

I was proud of him because he was up against men in their 30s and he believed this was the way to climb the ladder to get to where he was going. I have no doubt in my mind he would make it because he had the ambition and drive that made him shine. He was given a team that was at the bottom of the ladder the previous year and it was up to him to bring them to the top. This was all volunteer work and he believed this was the way to build his reputation; one he believed would make him reach his goals.

It's sad when I think Bryce knows nothing about his sons; he wouldn't even know what their favourite colour is or anything else about their lives. Parents should be part of a child's life forever, which makes me understand a lot about their past behaviours.

The eldest of the two boys never got into the police force and decided he wanted to become a builder. He was waiting for an interview with a school to see if he could get in. I was so worried about him as he had done so many courses, and I hoped this would be his chosen career. He may have been a late starter but sometimes it takes time to know the direction one needs to take.

I had no idea why he had been so lost and very different to his brother. This time, I hoped he would find what he loved. He had his real estate license and only lasted for a few months working for an agent but it wasn't for him. At least he had been studying. He was so much like me; he had no patience to give anything he tried time to work, to see the end results. He was my biggest worry as he continued down the path of immaturity and no self-worth. I could only hope and pray that he would find his feet.

Life had to move on for all of us. I had made up my mind that I was going to be a high achiever and set a great example for my boys. They were just so important to me. I had to get out and drop pamphlets more frequently on a daily basis and come up with some good promotional ideas.

I had to walk the talk, look the part, and stand out from the rest of the boys. Excitement was building within me; I felt like I was coming out of this deep depression that had been hanging over me like a dark cloud the past six years.

At an awards dinner I attended, the top achiever was a young man who grossed $300,000 commission for the year. I had to talk to him and find out how he got to that point, how long it took him. How much patience did I need to make it happen? I could feel the excitement of all the possibilities; I loved where I worked and that was a start as it had been so long since I had that feeling of enjoyment in the workplace. Still, it was only the beginning. The rest was up to me.

Soon after, I couldn't believe I saw Brad again, although it is a small town so I was bound to run into him from time to time. I had been in a prospective vendor's home and didn't realise she lived across the lake from his home. As I walked out to the backyard with the vendor, I could see his home and then I saw him looking back at me, although I am not sure he realised it was me. A flood of emotions come over me, but they were just emotions. This time, it was not only seeing him but seeing his home and where we used to sit, of seeing his boat and remembering the fun we used to have.

I had to remind myself this was a man whom I had trusted with my life, and had known for 27 years as a good friend. Complex feelings arose that night but I realised again it was just those old emotions triggering me to go back to that state of depression. I wouldn't allow myself to go there again, I was stronger than that.

No matter what, I would be happy because I was a survivor. If I worked really hard, I had to believe that I would soon be very successful. I kept telling myself that I don't need a man for my survival, I am who I am and I will be okay emotionally and financially. It truly is a mindset. Always remember what we think about, we bring about. I have seen enough evidence of that to know that is true.

Chapter 16

STRIVING FOR SUCCESS

Success is not all about money. Success is in every part of our lives and I wanted to achieve all of it in every area of my life, to become financially independent. I wanted to become the perfect mother and make up for all my mistakes I thought I had made. Wanted to have that picture perfect family I had yearned for ever since I was a little girl. I hungered for it.

Even though I knew I had accomplished so much in my life, it was just bits and pieces of my life, like a puzzle. There was no stability or continuity. Looking back, I felt I had sabotaged everything good that had tried to come into my life. Now, I had to ensure I made the right choices as I moved forward.

A new day. The beginning of the week, and I had made my mind up that I would achieve like no other.

There were two appointments I had to secure another two listings with John, and I was so excited to get to work. I set goals to work towards on a daily basis, reminding myself to work harder than I had ever worked in my life... although, as I said, nothing could be harder than the restaurant venture.

I had sent Bryce an email just to let him know our youngest son had finished his two-year diploma, in case he was interested. I thought it was the right thing to do because I still encouraged some sort of a relationship even though it always fell on deaf ears. One day, I know Bryce will regret not knowing his boys. The funny thing is, he thinks he has a relationship with them already but nothing could be farther from the truth.

Christmas was fast approaching and I needed to make it a special year because we had the worst Christmas the previous year. Time passes so quickly and so much had happened in the last 12 months, it was all so surreal. Even though I thought life had been cruel to me, I still had so much for which to be grateful. After all, I could have been homeless because of the restaurant fiasco. I just hoped I would find another property to live in before Christmas as I dreaded being where we were. It was a depressing place to be.

The week was nearly over and I had hoped to pick up a new listing but I didn't. I was feeling a bit flat. People are so strange, I had spent hours with one depressed woman who I really felt sorry for and she gave me every indication that she was going to let me sell her home but at the last minute she gave it to another agent, a man no less. I swear, I really don't get people sometimes. Why would they lead you up the garden path?

It was time to move on to the next one, and I kept

thinking about *The Law of Attraction*. I just knew I had to do better. That day, I had spoken to a recruitment person as I felt property management was where I needed to be and, strangely enough, if I had stuck out my job in property management 12 months prior, I would be moving into the townhouse I had bought off the plan the previous year. Nevertheless, it was too late; you just can't go back. I had to move on from the 'what ifs'.

I thought at least if I got a job in property management it would give me a steady income, and that's what I needed. My wages were just a retainer. In other words, once I got commission I would have to pay back John everything he had paid me. The weeks were dragging on, not to mention adding up. Up to that point, I owed John well over $3500. I had to do something, or I may end up with nothing and I couldn't afford to get to that point.

So much I had wanted this job to be great but it was not a busy office and there was another agent who was very popular in the area. It was very difficult, to say the least, but I had to keep trying.

Every day, I just wished my life would get better; meet someone nice and be financially independent, that's what I craved. The last six years were terrible and God certainly wasn't listening to me anymore. I needed him to hear me and give me a break. As the days went on, I found myself losing my faith. I was so stuck in this situation and I could not see the light at the end of the tunnel.

I was still looking for another rental and found a small house not far from where Bryce and I lived in our dream home. It was the right rental for me and I had to wait to see if I was approved. The property managers were so slow, and I couldn't understand why they had a great position and I couldn't get one. I appeared to be always waiting for something, which was a continual headache.

My eldest boy decided to get a tattoo even though he knew that I absolutely hated them. At first, he lied to me and said he didn't have it done but then whilst on Facebook, I came across the truth. It wasn't my place to tell him what to do at the age of nearly 22 but it was my business when I had bills piling up and he gave me nothing towards living expenses.

I was bewildered, and realised there was something very wrong with this picture. What had I taught him? Why did he not have the need to be responsible? I was disappointed and continued to blame myself for the way he was because I was the parent and I took my role seriously. Some would have said, kick him out. After all, he had caused me so much heartache over the years; however, I knew who he was underneath. He was and is a wonderful, compassionate, misunderstood person. He needs confidence and he does not realise his full potential. It was never meant to be this way, and I couldn't tell anyone how lost and lonely I felt. No one to speak to, no one to help me turn my life around, and I started to feel sick. Really sick. I think it must have been stress but at that point, I didn't care. I had enough of life and I didn't believe I had enjoyed it at all.

From the age of 17, my life had always belonged to someone else. It was never about me, and I sacrificed so much to give to all my children – although my two eldest would not agree with that statement. I had to keep in the top of mind, 'whatever doesn't destroy us makes us stronger'.

I had to get over the way I was feeling and jump back on the listing trail in my job. To continue my pursuit of happiness and believe it would change for the better if I was to survive.

One particular day was so much better than any other, and I thought if only it could be like that every day I would never leave my job. I had a buyer for a unit I had listed but I couldn't sign them up as there was no section 32, so I had to wait till the following Monday and hopefully they wouldn't change their minds. Then I had some other people interested in three other properties. I was so excited, and thought that if they all wanted to buy, that would give me a great start in real estate. Give me so much confidence. I felt things were starting to move and couldn't wait till the next week to get the sale.

In the meantime, I had a call from Melissa who was from a recruitment agency. She said she would meet with me the following week. I had to cover all my bases but I didn't want to make any mistakes like I had previously. When it came down to it, I knew if I had the choice, I wanted to stay in my job and be successful. Stay positive. Make it happen. I needed to believe in myself and have faith it would work out the way it was meant to – to have purpose and financial independence.

My deal came together; I was so excited. My first sale! I got both commissions as the lister and the salesperson, which gave me 40% of the commission. It was a fantastic feeling!

Then there was the reality check. I wasn't going to see that money. There was only enough to pay back what John had already paid me as a retainer. That part that was the hardest. It was the first job, and as I said, I really enjoyed it, but there wasn't nearly enough money and I wasn't a patient person when it came to money.

It was time to meet with the recruitment company and I had decided this time to exaggerate how long I had been in my current position. I had always been honest and it got me nowhere. If I wanted to get further, I couldn't tell the truth this time. The position for which I had the interview was a 40-minute drive from home, but the position as a senior property manager was one I wanted. It was with a very reputable company that paid well. I got through the interview and they rang not long after to ask if I would meet with the CEO the next day.

Nerves hit me because when you tell one lie the rest

of the lies follow. Please remember, I had to survive and it was my way... or no way was I going to get the job. I had applied for over 100 positions and no one cared how much trouble I went to, no acknowledgement at all. They call themselves recruitment companies, they say 'we want you' in their advertisements but it's all just lies. They treat you like crap and don't care at all. Not even just to send you a letter thanking you for sending your resume. I feel so sorry for anyone trying to get a position in today's world.

At the same time, I was served with a notice to quit, which meant I had to leave the home I was renting within 60 days because relatives of the landlord were moving in. Even though I wanted to move anyway and was just waiting on approval for another property to rent, this was the universe's way of moving me on.

Then I received a letter from a debt collector, which was a bit frightening and I had to wait till the next day to find out what that was about. Obviously, the restaurant and an account that was not paid.

It was all getting too much and I knew I really didn't want to leave my job. Patience was all that was required, and a bit of front. I had a call from the recruitment company again to inform me the CEO I had seen was very interested in me. Shock doesn't begin to cover how I felt. It had been years I had been waiting for someone to say that, for a dream job paying what I wanted. I realised maybe I was not doing the right thing for me and went to my boss, John.

I asked him if he could make my retainer a little more and he agreed, so I stayed. He had so much faith in me and I decided that I would be far better off where I was. Besides, the more money I got, the more I was taxed. Then there was travelling expenses. It wasn't worth it. John had given me a chance that no one else had – the possibility to earn big money. All I had to do was get more confident, which is what I planned to do. I was going to be a success and I wanted it so bad. It was all I thought about. I had to work hard to attain my dream, and I was prepared to do just that.

Chapter 17

KEEPING FAITH

Who remembers hearing, 'every day in every way I will get better and better'? It is an old saying that I always loved, and I would tell myself that every morning. Every time I dropped pamphlets in letterboxes for the business, I would repeatedly say: 'listings come easy to me' until they did. I wasn't about to let anything or anyone stand in my way.

My family was a mess and my work was all I had. More importantly, I had come to realise I couldn't change the way my eldest children felt about me. That was just the way it was. My youngest boys were the only ones I knew I could depend on from time to time. The difference was, between them and my eldest two, they always got over our spats. We said what we had to say and then we would move on, which is the way it should be.

The boys and I had realised there was only the three of us. We had no one else to depend on, we were the family. My mum was always there as well, so it was time to put what *had been* the family, behind me and start over.

I had to concentrate on becoming a success and stop allowing thoughts of my family problems to disrupt my thinking. If I wanted to be a success, I had to stay focused and get rid of the disappointment I felt for my eldest children and their spouses.

In my own mind, once I moved house it would all fall into place. The real estate agent still had no answer for me and I was getting frustrated by the continual wait. It was as if the place I had been living refused to let me go. I had always believed it was full of bad karma because it was built on Aboriginal ground, and nothing good had happened there. In fact, just the opposite. It had been the worst 16 months of my entire life. Even worse than those bad relationships.

I continued packing as I knew the coming week I should hear something. It was another birthday and I was overdue for the next seven years of my life to begin. Isn't that what they say? Every seven years your life changes? It all had to change. God knows, it just had to. The cost of rental properties was ridiculously high. I couldn't comprehend how a normal family survived in today's world. What was ahead for my boys? Were they always going to live with me? How do young people move forward in today's world? My concern is probably the same as many parents around the world, because life wasn't what it used to be and it is always much more difficult being a single parent.

Confidence and excitement were starting to build in me, knowing that I was leaving the townhouse to a new place where happiness was awaiting me. Many will say happiness is within but sometimes it is also about your surroundings.

I knew in my heart that my birthday was a new beginning and I would leave behind all the bad stuff. My youngest had an interview with a university on my birthday and I just knew it was going to be good. My other son was waiting to be accepted for his building course and I knew that would happen as well because he always was a practical person, not a studious one and was always meant to have a trade. My boys were polar opposites, and all I wanted for them was success and to be able to live a good life and survive in today's world comfortably.

Then and only then would I feel true happiness. I knew in my heart even though over those years I had so many issues of my own to deal with, they knew I had done a great job as a mother.

There was still had no news from the property manager about the rental I so badly wanted and was getting rather anxious not knowing where I was going. My heart kept telling me to move closer to my daughter in Berwick, although I knew that would be a disaster. She had shown no concern for me as I was going through the restaurant fiasco. My boys wanted to stay close to their friends and I just couldn't see harmony if I moved away... although, I believed it may have been best for them away from the alcohol and from the influence of some not-so-great friends who seemed to party all the time.

I was totally over the drinking and kids not taking responsibility for themselves at their age. When I think back to the way kids were years ago, it really frustrated me. They just never seemed to stand on their own two feet and constantly became a burden. My boys needed to become men.

It had been one of the loneliest weekends I had encountered and I really felt so isolated. No one cared and Christmas was coming. I had to get out of this state of mind, and packing was probably the best way to keep me occupied.

There was no choice but to be ready just in case I was lucky enough to get the home I applied for. I wasn't sure what I was going to do if I missed out. Keep my faith, that's all I could do, and hope that all would work out in the end.

My job with John was going slow and I had to remember it was Christmas so I needed to give it till February just to make sure it wasn't going to work for me. Other people made it work, and I continually told myself it should be the same for me.

I just couldn't accept that nothing was working in my life. Why? I didn't understand. What did I ever do to anyone? Yet here I was facing all sorts of problems. I had to learn patience and discipline if I was to rise above it all. Those two words I never understood.

A rather disturbing letter from the man I had bought the restaurant from, arrived, asking me for a few thousand dollars, which was outrageous. It had been sent from his lawyer. I couldn't believe the gall of this man who had totally ripped me off. He maintained that I owed him for stock and wages, which was absurd. I sent an email to his lawyer telling him to take me to court, as I owed nothing and believed me no man was going to rip me off again. Had I been cursed? How much bad luck could I have? I couldn't understand why this was happening to me.

Was I playing the victim? Is that why all these nasty things were happening? Or, was it the horrible, unlucky home I lived in? Whatever the reason, it was totally unfair, so I had to find a way of ignoring everything. Including both my sons' behaviour of late. Every weekend they were partying. They seemed to be going back to their old ways and I had just about had enough. I never understood the way they thought when they saw what I was facing.

I started reading *Follow Your Heart* by Andrew Matthews. Funnily enough, it had been sitting next to my bed for months. It was the only book I had not packed away or read. I think I must have bought it years prior and it just sat in my bookcase for some reason. Things happen for a reason, and I believe the same for books. Maybe there was a reason I was only reading it now.

The book was about believing in yourself, and I realised I needed to stay optimistic no matter how bleak things may have looked. *Follow Your Heart* was the reinforcement I was looking for and I knew I just had to believe that eventually everything would start to change for the better.

Even though I said I was going to give my job with John till February, another position had come up that was a 50-minute drive from home, and I was lucky enough to get an interview. The opportunity was too good to miss. Financially, it would help me get my own home over the next 12 months. That was the most important thing to me. I really needed that security.

I finally heard from the property manager that I was the successful applicant for the rental. It was all happening. I felt I owed a lot to the book *Follow Your Heart*, because I was changing my thoughts. However, all the pressure was on me when I was told I could move into the property on Christmas Eve.

This was going to be hard because there was only me. No one to help, and I was alone. The boys helped me a little but then took off for the weekend again, out of control. I had to get the packing done but my depression got the better of me and I started drinking – the worst thing I could have done.

When one goes down this pathetic path it's because of the loneliness, of having no one to turn to. The next day, I pulled myself together and continued reading this fabulous book, which somehow gave me the strength I needed to get through the next week. Pack the house, get the position I applied for, and move into my new home. It was all going to happen, and from that point on I knew all would start to become normal again in my life.

It had been six years since there was any form of normality for me. I started feeling everything would be okay, and that when I settled in the new rental that maybe I would take up a hobby. Golf, perhaps, with my eldest of the two boys. He was my biggest worry, and he needed that closeness because Bryce was never going to be there for him.

I wanted and needed their lives to become normal because it had broken my heart over the years to see their lives in such turmoil. The only real family they had was their nana and me.

Their sister was there occasionally, and their eldest brother and his family had disowned us all even at Christmas. Including my poor mum. I had asked myself repeatedly why or how could this be?

They had disowned us the Christmas prior and had only come back when they wanted me to buy the restaurant, which is where all my troubles started. Families, as I said earlier, should be there for each other no matter what. I can't say that enough, and I had always believed in unconditional love.

Everyone makes mistakes, even those closest to you. My eldest and his wife had been so horrible with the restaurant fiasco but what could I do? They just turned their backs on all of us. My eldest son and his wife had forgotten if it had not been for Bryce, they would not have had their first home. We helped them so much in the past financially but, conveniently, they had forgotten that too.

I have to say Bryce was always good to my eldest son, even more so than his own father. My daughter was the only one who was always self-sufficient. I never had a worry with her. As I said, I maintain that love is unconditional and if you learn from your mistakes that is all that matters. Everyone should be able to still move on and continue to be a family. No one should sit in judgment of others!

I had become bitter because of my situation and knew I just had to concentrate on the boys and our new life. This was to be the week that everything changed for the better, starting with getting this new position.

Then I got an email to say the position would not become available for another month, which gave me time to give my sales job with John a chance. I wasn't sure at this stage whether I would even get a second interview, so decided if it was meant to be it would be.

I kept moving forward, and we moved into a great house, which we all felt had good karma. I can't explain why. It just felt good, and the boys felt it too. Once I was unpacked, it felt like home. I even unpacked boxes that had not been opened for years. Placed my family photos on the walls and just sat in awe. It felt so right.

Funnily, I was reading my star sign and it said I was moving to a place that made me feel like I was coming home. That's exactly how I felt. Every day I wished I had the money to purchase the home, although it was not for sale. I felt like we were meant to be here, and it was just down the road from where my youngest boys went to kindergarten. It was also around the corner from where Bryce and I had built our first home.

So many memories. Maybe too close to home but, still, in many ways comforting.

Chapter 18

GOOD KARMA

Christmas was here, and it had to mean 2011 was going to be different from the previous year when the boys and I sat alone and had no one to share the festive season with. Everything was about to change. I just had that feeling.

My eldest sister had rung me the night before Christmas and asked the boys and me to celebrate the day with her family. I knew my youngest sister was going and she hadn't spoken to me for nearly 30 years, so I was hesitant. The last thing I wanted was to put a damper on the day for everyone else. I had no idea why she hated me all those years. All I knew is that it started the day I left my first husband. No matter what we went through as kids, my sisters and I had a reasonably close relationship growing up but our family situation had affected us in different ways through Dad's drinking.

Even when our kids were little, we always looked after each other's children. We were all I thought quite close. My dad had always said to me that it was jealousy, and even though our family was dysfunctional because of alcohol, we were still close-knit.

I had tried several times to make it right with her but

she never wanted anything to do with me. Over the years, I just accepted the way it was. When my father died, I was resentful towards her as I felt she had robbed him of his family, which I knew would have made him a very happy man had it all been resolved. It affects all of the family when one person creates such disharmony; at Christmas, birthdays and other special occasions. It is so wrong when families are torn apart because of another's selfishness. It ends up hurting everyone for no reason. On the other hand, I suppose we do not know what others are going through and she had many of her own problems. If families communicated, no one would ever be in these types of situations. As my mum always taught me, say what you think and get over it. It sounds so easy but I suppose it is not.

So, I decided to go to my sister's family Christmas. Why should I be alone again? I needed and wanted them in my life. The boys and I always enjoyed spending time with them. My sister had a beautiful family and they were so close even though her husband had passed away seven years prior. He was a wonderful man and I think anyone that had known him still misses him to this day. He had died far too young and was the most amazing man, father, and husband.

The day started off great; my eldest son of the two youngest brought me breakfast in bed, which delighted me. He made me feel so special. Then we had our own special morning together around the Christmas tree.

Next, it was off to my sister's festive Christmas and we were all so happy to be there. She and her family had gone to so much trouble for everyone.

I walked in and my youngest sister was there; not a word was spoken between us. We had lunch and then gave out presents, although I had nothing for anyone except my mum. That was okay because we had decided not to exchange gifts. My nephew, who was playing Father Christmas, handed me a present but I didn't have my glasses on and could barely see who it was from. So I asked my son to read it to me and was shocked that it was from my youngest sister. I opened the present to find lovely gold earrings she had bought me. I can't tell you how I felt at that stage. It just blew me away, and I had so many mixed emotions that brought tears to my eyes.

The war was finally over.

I waited until she was alone, walked up to her and asked the obvious question: why had she bought me a gift?

Her reply was, "It's about time, isn't it?"

I told her I had nothing for her, and she said it didn't matter, so I kissed her and left it at that.

We didn't speak after that, and I didn't want to push it. It had been nearly 30 years and the relationship had to repair slowly. I haven't heard from her since but I am sure that we are both on the path to recovery. I just wish it had been when Dad was alive; I know Mum was so happy that she got to see it.

So you see, there is no reason to hold grudges in life, no matter the reason.

When you are a family, it should go without saying. We should never sit in judgement of others; we may not agree with what others do, as that is their choice. Who are we to say what is right and what is wrong? We all make our own life choices and we have to live with them but it should not affect or infect our lives with each other.

I feel I have grown so much these past six years since I asked Bryce to leave, even though they have been the worst years I have known. Maybe that is why I am alone, to understand more about who I am. Although, I still don't understand why we have to go through so much pain when we are learning our life lessons.

It had been the best Christmas Day the boys and I had known for years. My family was getting back on track even though my eldest son had disowned us. He had his own lessons to learn but I felt it didn't matter anymore; we all have the journey of life's lessons and his was no different. I could do nothing about it and had, by this stage, accepted his family's decision to disown us, although it was sad for my grandchildren.

They were the ones that would suffer because of it. Two beautiful young girls who were 13 and 10 years old did not need this hostility in their lives. My son and his wife were not teaching them about love or forgiveness – all they were teaching them was anger and hatred.

One thing I know for sure is that he will have so many regrets one day for the years he lost with his extended family. And all for what?

It seemed I had gained a sister and lost a son. That didn't make any sense to me at all but there was nothing I could do to change the situation. I had texted my son twice before Christmas to put an end to the animosity but got no reply, so I had done all I could.

Life is a circle of change. Sometimes, it is out of our control so we just have to live with the choices that people make and accept them. I think that is what I have learned; the more you fight against the situation the worse it becomes, but when you accept where you are in life, it becomes easier to live with.

New Years Eve was upon us and there was no one at home. The boys had gone on separate road trips with their friends and I was alone again. I decided to take the time and reflect on the past and try to make sense of it. Ridiculous, of course, but I started watching all the home videos Bryce had made with his movie camera. I hadn't had the camera out of the box for years and I wanted to go down memory lane. It was both funny and sad. It was a life I realised that was a happy one at times. There was no doubt in my mind watching the boys with their dad in the videos that there were some really happy moments. No one could take those memories from me.

What I learned whilst watching them was that even

though Bryce was unfaithful so many times, I had to question myself. What part did I play in the demise of our marriage? I knew his infidelity was not because of anything I had done. He had always been that way, even before I had met him. Still, I should not have looked at that as an excuse for drinking too much. It never helped anything, just made it all so much worse.

I am not excusing his behaviour, which I think led to my drinking but, at some point, you have to question the part one plays in the demise of a relationship.

It made me realise that if we had both tried, and he could have focused on his family, we would have had a great life together. The boys would have been different. They would have been more confident and secure in their lives, which would have made a huge difference to them both. My eldest of the two would not have so much anger in him, and they both would have had stable lives.

My reflection was well worth it because it showed me that we were still a family whether Bryce was with us or not. I sent him a text on New Year's Eve saying to him that I had been watching our home videos and he was a great dad when the boys were small and my wish for him was that he could have a close relationship with his sons again if he wanted. It did not have to be this way. They were not close at all and even though he had remarried, it should not make any difference.

Dads are so important in their son's eyes. They look

to their dad as their role model. Boys watch and listen to everything their daddy says and does. That becomes the end product, a chip off the old block, so maybe now I should be saying just as well they didn't have that at all.

I probably shouldn't say that, because Bryce could have taught his sons things that would have made a huge difference to them.

I wanted that so much for our boys, as they had been cheated by not having their dad in their lives, especially with Bryce living in Queensland. Hopefully, one day, they will mend and be together again.

It is hard to undo the past but we can change the future at any time. Just a word or gesture makes all the difference. Every child needs the love of their parents, no matter how old they are. We all suffer and carry with us the rejection we feel through our journey in life.

New Year's Eve was hard but I am so grateful that I am where I am. It will only get better from here. Giving is the answer for all of us in life. It is not what we get but about what we give. It is not about what happens to us, it is how we deal with it.

There are always those less fortunate in the world who have severe problems but it does not make our own lives any less painful by realising that either. Maybe awareness is the word I am looking for because when we are aware of what is going on around us in the world, we become more grateful for what we have.

Chapter 19

THE YEAR AHEAD

Optimism is what I needed to focus on and I relied on my wonderful books to help me keep on track. There was no way I was going to allow myself to be stuck in life's vicious circle again. It was full steam ahead from this point and I was ready for the year ahead.

I sent my youngest sister a Happy New Year message. I thought it would be small steps to get us back on track and her reply was good. This was the beginning to getting our family back together. At this stage, I felt there was nothing I could not achieve. My family was the most important to me and I knew going back to the beginning was right; establishing the relationships that were lost somewhere in the last 30 years.

Watching the home videos on New Year's Eve made me homesick for Bryce. He was a great dad when the boys were little, and I knew he could be again. If he only just realised what he was missing. I only wished we could have made it work, that he had not been so unfaithful to us all. We were great at times but there was no point looking back; he was married now and life would never be the same anyway.

Once the trust is gone, there is no way you can repair a relationship. I knew that because I had taken Bryce back in 1992. At the time, I was kidding myself. I thought I could rebuild that trust but realistically, you never can. Once the circle of trust is broken, you can never go back. In saying that, I have to remember there are those I have known who have mended their relationships. However, if they were truly honest, I am sure they will never forget the betrayal, that every now and again they find themselves mistrusting.

It is something that never truly leaves you.

I realised I had been mourning the past six years. When someone dies, you can't get them back. It doesn't matter what we think and how much we wanted it to turn out differently, what's done is done.

Often, I wonder if he thinks of us, whether he misses us as a family or even cares. It would be nice to know. I truly loved him back then and he will never know how his actions hurt us all, particularly our sons. It breaks my heart to think I was never enough. Realistically, the grass is never greener on the other side. Eventually, he will have karma as I did. So will Brad.

No one goes without learning eventually that life's mistakes come back to us. I often wondered if Bryce had regrets. Maybe, maybe not. Was he a callous, shallow person? Who knows? Those are the unanswered questions I will take to my grave. But I loved him, and will probably never love anyone else that way again. We were together 22 years.

You so often hear about men leaving their wives after they have been married 25 years, and I will never understand that. They should be best friends. How could someone leave their best friend for someone they hardly know? Unless, of course, they had good reason. Most of the time though, it is just because of lust.

Bryce missed out on so much, whether he knows it or not. His children in their teens, the family, and the wonderful moments I was so privileged to have. He missed it all, and even though there have been so many problems with the boys, there have also been wonderful times too.

No one can get those moments back. I wonder if he ever thinks about the time he missed his youngest son's first steps and his first birthday party all those years ago in 1992 when he left us the very first time. He missed celebrating all their birthdays and every Christmas for the last six years, I cannot for the life of me comprehend how any man can just put their children to one side and not give them another thought. It is beyond comprehension!

I would not trade for the world, those magical moments, warts and all.

My younger boys had, over the years, shown me such love even though they had given me grief and of late and returned to their bad habits. I don't know why they are continually in this party frame of mind with no responsibility. Perhaps it is the new generation.

I don't know how to change anything right now so I just ride the storm as usual. The more I fight with them about their behaviour, the worse it gets; so, it is best left alone. However, they should have part-time or at least casual jobs at their age whilst they are studying.

As a parent, I know I am not the only one who has this problem; they just seem to lack responsibility for themselves. Still, they are in their 20s.

I emailed Bryce this morning just to ask his advice; I wanted him to understand that our boys were heading on this path of destruction and I needed his help. I didn't expect him to come to the rescue but he was still their dad and he hadn't seen his youngest for so long, and who was at this stage becoming the worst of the two with alcohol. Alcoholism ran in our genes but it wasn't just that it was the way young ones were today, it's a different world.

Bryce replied to my email and for the first time acknowledged my situation. He said I should get a one-bedroom unit and then the boys would have no choice but to live on their own.

Quite true, but so unrealistic! I could never see my sons on the street, and I realise it may be easy for some to do that but not for me. I am a mother and they are my children, even if they were adults. I needed to find another way to bring them to their senses.

I had been watching the series *Brothers and Sisters*. The

boys had given me the box set for Christmas and it made me realise I did not have a crazy family. The mother in the series was no different to me but my family was. The family in the series argued a lot but got over their arguments and still loved each other. This was the way my mother had raised me; however, in my family they just didn't get over their arguments. They hung on to every word that was said. At least that was the case with the eldest two from my first marriage, who both continued to make my family dysfunctional.

My eldest son and daughter had so much jealousy all these years for the youngest two. Our family was never going to be like the Walkers on the series, which was really sad.

It should not make a difference how many children are in a family, how many fathers there are, or how much age difference there is between them. They all still should love each other and be there for each other. That was my impression of my perfect family, and I blamed my eldest two for making it the way it was.

I knew that my family would never change. It had been like this since the boys were born and there was nothing I could do about it. The eldest two always picked on my mistakes and believed I loved the youngest two more, which was not true. However, I had come to resent the eldest two for not allowing our family to be just that – a family.

It was Sunday morning and I woke to find my youngest had not come home. I had come to the stage of always saying to myself that no news is good news but it wasn't easy. At least if they had their own place, I would get used to that and I would stop worrying whether they were okay.

I awoke depressed thinking about the lost girl on her 17th birthday finding out she was pregnant all those years ago and the sacrifices she had made. It was like thinking of someone else rather than realising it was me.

Even back then, I had a choice; I didn't have to go through with having a child but I did. I was such a naïve girl and we were not educated about sex like the kids are today. My eldest children's father was my first sexual experience. He was as naïve as me and, as they say, the rest is history.

I felt cheated out of a life; I didn't know what it was like to be a teenager or fulfil my dreams to be an actress or even a lawyer. Ever since I can remember, those were the two professions I had wished for when growing up. Had my head been screwed on properly, I could have gone back to school after I had my first baby, but I didn't. What I am saying is, that life is a choice and no matter what happens to us we do have a choice if we stay focused on our own lives. I didn't have to give up my dreams, I could have still pursued them and life would have been very different for me. It was always about someone else, looking after everyone except my needs and me. That is what most mothers do without realising, and then it is too late.

I am at the point now where I need to think of my life with just me in it because all my children—even though I still have two at home—they had their own lives and I was on the outer.

My focus had to be on where I was going and to accept that I was alone.

I knew that my eldest two were very close, and my eldest son and daughter-in-law were the cause of my isolation from family. My daughter was very close to them and it was obvious she had no loyalty to me. She believed nothing I said. My daughter-in-law had poisoned her mind against me. There was nothing I could do, or wanted to do by this time, I just had to accept they were all out of my life.

As a mother, I did the best I could and there was no way I could fix anything without being accused of having an ulterior motive. I was, and am, a big believer in loyalty to one's family; it wasn't that I wanted anyone to take sides, I just wanted them to believe my side of the story with the restaurant fiasco. No one ever did.

Why would my own daughter believe my daughter-in-law over me? Everything that came out of her mouth was a lie. She was the one who made my life a living hell when we were in the restaurant and destroyed my family along with my eldest son. I do believe in karma and I know one day the truth will come out. It was strange to think of my daughter-in-law that way because I thought we were close at one time but I suppose you never really know anyone.

I had not heard from the companies with whom I had second interviews, and I hoped that would change soon. It had given me enough time to appreciate where I was with John, selling real estate.

I had never stayed long enough to see if I could make it in previous positions. Now, I had time on my side to make the right decision on where I was meant to be. I really enjoyed working for John and his personal assistant. They had become like family even though we were all so totally different. When I think about it, I believe it was because we didn't judge each other and criticize each other for anything.

In the last two months, I had listed and sold one property but keep in mind it was the Christmas period; it wasn't a clear indication of what could be. With the book *The Secret*, sitting next to my bed, I just knew it may be worth hanging on for a while. I really believed in the power of the mind. I knew now was the time to put to the test what *The Secret* had been telling me, and becoming patient was a big part of that.

I needed to build relationships in the community, stay focused, work hard and believe success was not too far away.

Often, I wondered how I had come to where I was living and working and had realised three years prior I had looked to buy the home I was living in at the same time I had dropped my résumé into the real estate office I was working at.

At that time, I could have bought the home I am now living in but thought the backyard was too small. I never heard from the real estate agent back then about my résumé, but here I was in the now and for some unexplainable reason, I was where I was meant to be. John had bought the real estate office three years after I had submitted my résumé. It all had to mean something. Life is full of unknown messages and if I didn't believe it then, I certainly do now. Instincts also play a very big part in one's life and where you end up. Successful people use their instincts.

My life had not been kind to me for many reasons, even though I had made so many sacrifices. Writing this book has enabled me to keep my sanity.

Writing about everything that had happened to me was confronting and I was able to understand it so much more clearly. It has been an amazing journey for me to be able to take a closer look at myself because there is so much to understand about why we are so driven by emotions.

I became preoccupied and worried about one of my sons who had started seeing a woman 12 years his senior and with two children. Worried about history repeating itself but there was nothing I could do.

When Bryce and I started dating, no one could have told me to stop seeing him. I was so in love. With my son, I had to let go and let him make his own mistakes whether I agreed or not. I had no control over that situation.

He was such an angry young man and, if I were to be honest, he was the worry of my life but there was no way I was going to interfere. Now, I appreciate how Bryce's mum and dad must have felt when his son of 20 was going out with a woman of 28 with two children. They must have been horrified.

I could never understand why they were so upset, but I do now.

That's what happens to all of us on our life journey. We understand very little when we are younger but, as you age, you do have a better understanding of how parents felt when we thought we knew it all. Especially when it happens to us. We become the parents. All of a sudden, we are learning.

Fortunately, the relationship between my son and the older woman fizzled out and I felt relieved to say the least.

It is sad, really, because we never get how someone else feels until it happens to us. I suppose that is how life is. For my sons, I wanted normality, which is probably what Bryce's parents wanted for him. It would be nice to be able to tell them that I understand now but it is too late.

They have both passed on. Yet another lesson for me!

That's what life teaches us; never wait to say the things you want to say to anyone. Particularly those you love. It's too late when they are gone.

Life is about lessons as we get older and some things are just too hard to learn but we have to whether we like it or not. I am told that our lessons in life keep repeating themselves until we understand what they are meant to teach us. I now get it!

I needed to let my younger boys go, let them find their own lives. No longer was I in control. I just hoped it would turn out right for all of us. We were in a good place, the home we lived in did have good karma and it was a nice feeling.

There was a lot riding on the following week, to see if I could make it in real estate. This time, I had a good feeling about it.

Chapter 20

DREAMS BECOME REALITY

My week went well. I now had four listings on the board and I was so excited. I started to see the bigger picture and knew I was where I was meant to be. It was all falling into place. It's true what they say with everything we do, you have to put in the hard yards to see results.

My eldest of the two boys, or should I say men, by this time was starting his pre-apprentice course in building and my youngest was accepted into university to become a PE teacher for secondary and primary. I was over the moon, and I have to say that is when any mother or father who has done it on their own can say it was all worth it. Maybe now the boys would settle down and have the opportunity for their lives to come together, to put all the anger behind them.

As I said, I knew they loved me and I knew eventually they would find their lives, have great careers and perhaps grow a wonderful family themselves. I knew without a doubt that they would make great dads because they knew from looking at their own father that they could never put anyone through what they had to endure.

I realised at this point that this was going to be the

hardest challenge of my life. My eldest children had deserted me and I didn't know whether they would ever come back into my life.

Financially, it was now or never; I had to make it work. I was grateful my youngest boys were starting a new chapter in their lives, as we all had to move on. Maybe some normality for them but I was still the one who had to deliver financially and that had been a struggle in itself.

I had picked up another two listings but knew that wasn't enough. So, every day I would drop pamphlets and make calls. I needed to make some sales. Within myself, I knew it was now all achievable but it would not happen overnight. The end result was up to me. There was no one else. If it was going to be, it was up to me.

Exhausted, I was working six days a week but I had to keep going. It's an awful feeling when there is no one to share all the burdens with. I think so many couples take for granted what they have because when you are on your own it's just you and only you that have to be the responsible one for everyone and everything.

Finally, I made another sale. There was not much commission in it for me because it was another office's referral but nevertheless, it was a sale. I felt I was moving forward. Very slowly but still, forward momentum. At least the signs were there. I was not about to give up. It was only a matter of time before I would get on my feet. It was hard to stay positive knowing my eldest son and daughter wanted nothing to do with me. On occasion, I felt myself slipping into a depression but somehow always managed to pull myself up.

Every time those emotions rose, I told myself that it was *just* emotions. As I have said so many times, it is not what happens to you but how you deal with it. This was the way I had conditioned myself to deal with my thoughts.

I knew I had to say 'stop' every time I felt myself going under. It seemed to be working. I was starting to focus on my job and by this time I really loved where I was working.

It's funny how certain people come into our lives to give us more information than we bargained for.

One of our landlords came in and the irony of it was that Bryce had worked with her many years prior. She had recognised me from when I was on Council and knew that I was Bryce's ex-wife.

She spoke about Bryce and how she knew him, which was not flattering to him at all. He was worse than I had thought, which took me back to a place I didn't want to remember. The memories were hard enough but to know he was such a womaniser was incredibly degrading to me. As she said, he was such a manipulator.

It's true that sometimes the people that work with your partner in life know so much more about your life than you do! I shrugged it off and knew I was not going to let it get under my skin... although, it did at first. Once again, I thought I had come to terms with the man I had known for 22 years but in actual fact, I didn't know him at all. It just seemed all so surreal.

I had a call from another potential client and this time it was an up-market property in the marina. So much excitement! Another listing I badly wanted.

The vendor had several agents giving appraisals and I just kept saying to myself that I would be the winner in the end. Keeping a positive mind is one of the most powerful tools you can have. It paid off. The vendor rang just before I was about to leave the office one afternoon and he told me I was the most professional. He gave me the listing. The property was absolutely beautiful and worth about 1.2 million dollars. I was over the moon. My listings were growing and I knew the sales would come.

This was a pivotal moment in my working life. I had come to realise the two major lessons I had not learned were here to teach me – discipline and patience. I had never stayed anywhere long enough the last six years to give anything time to work, and maybe I had never really worked hard enough. I expected it would all just come to me and if it didn't happen quickly then I had the mindset that it wasn't going to happen at all. Not once had I thought of myself as lazy. so maybe it was due to the lack of confidence that had been stripped away from me piece by piece over the years.

If I didn't have confidence in a sales role, how could anyone else believe in me?

I had never had a problem with confidence in my professional life before I went into Council as an elected member. From that moment when I left the newspaper along with everything that happened with Bryce, my life started to crumble around me. It was the beginning of losing all my self-confidence both personally and professionally.

That day, I felt the happiest I had for some time, realising my professional life was moving forward. I had to focus on getting to the top of my career and not allow my personal issues to get in the way.

I was starting to believe in who I was and looked forward to pursuing my goals. You see, I wasn't just another real estate salesperson, I cared about the people I met. Treated them the way I liked to be treated. I believed in honesty and always doing what was right for my vendors. I didn't cut corners or look at people like some agents did as just another client.

In the meantime, I had a crisis at home. My eldest of the two boys was not doing well. I didn't realise for some time that he had gone back to his old ways, drinking too much alcohol. I couldn't understand why he would go back to this when his life was finally coming together. He had thrown one of his tantrums and started lashing out, which is when I realised I had a real problem. I had to try to get through to him but I didn't know how. Alcohol affects every person differently. He was one of those people who get so very angry, and the language was what no mother should have to endure. I thought we were all on the same page and everyone was getting their lives on track. As much as I was hurt and angry, I had to find a way to help him.

I really couldn't understand his behaviour; he was nearly 22 years of age and had put my youngest and I through so much. There were moments where I was reliving my childhood, and I didn't deserve that.

Alcoholism is bad enough and when mixed with other substances it is so much worse. He should have been happy but didn't realise that going down this path was not going to allow him to see happiness or success.

How was I going to help him? I didn't know, and felt he was on a path of destruction. At this point, I had to think of my youngest. I had hardened up a little and he wasn't going to stay with me if he couldn't change. He needed to see a doctor and work out what was going on. Of course, he wouldn't and if I pushed the point, he would lash out at me. I had become frightened by this stage because his temper was the worst I had ever lived with, and I found myself becoming frightened like a child.

I deserved better.

I had done everything for my children... except, they weren't children anymore. Yet here I was still looking after them at the age of 20 and 22. I knew there was something wrong with that picture. My eldest two were out of home by the time they were 18. There is a lot to be said about the different generations, and that is definitely what they were.

They didn't even pay board; they didn't get it at all. Maybe it was my fault because I had always done so much for them. They never went without. Didn't know what it was to work hard either. Although, my youngest at least had casuals jobs on the odd occasion.

I thought I was doing all the right things as a parent but maybe I was making my own situation worse. It was time to examine the part I had played in all of it. As the old saying goes, you have to be cruel to be kind... but I could never be that cruel person, which was my downfall.

When I looked to Bryce for help, he was not interested at all. So, I had no choice but to deal with it myself.

Chapter 21

GETTING BACK ON TRACK

I felt so overwhelmed by this stage and yet I knew I had to stay focused. Couldn't allow the issues with my son to take me back to the space I had been. He could change if I found a way to get through to him. I had decided I would give him an ultimatum – either he got off the substances he was taking or he would have to move out.

There was fear in doing that because I knew I could make the situation so much worse. However, to me, this was making him responsible for his own life and his own choices. I had always believed in taking responsibility for the choices one makes in life and this was no different. There is accountability for everyone and at this stage, he had to know that.

I couldn't keep helping him and covering up his mistakes. No longer would I put up with anymore abuse in my life. It just had to be over.

It only takes one person to upset a family and I had so many disappointments with most of my children. Surely, I had the power to make it change. So much for the perfect family I had always dreamt of ever since I was a child. At this stage, I didn't know whether it would ever happen, if everyone would ever live a normal happy life. I felt like a failure but I knew I had done the best I could at the time.

I started thinking of the past, which I did so often trying to make sense of my life. It was then I realised had I stayed in my marriage the first time, I would have been married 39 years. I will never forget being that naive girl of just 17, giving up my life to become a mother. Now, looking back, I don't know where all the years went and still no life of my own. I could never have a normal relationship with anyone again even if I wanted to. Not as long as I was living in a situation filled with problems.

Still, I really didn't care. My closest friend lived in Brisbane, and she had been on her own for 16 years. She had the occasional relationship but nothing really serious until now. She had given up on anyone coming into her life and wasn't looking to be with another man.

Andrea had a great job and her own home, she didn't need anyone in her life but then life presented her with a guy she has now been with for some time. She had met him years prior but for some reason had never taken an interest; maybe the time wasn't right back then. She had two boys of her own and had gone through her own heartache but once she had dealt with all of that and had total independence, her life changed. Maybe there was hope for me yet.

I couldn't think about meeting anyone. Not when I had

to get my son back on track and focus on my job. Nothing was going to hold me back and I wasn't about to lose my son to a society of mixed-up kids.

He had to change. I had to have faith. There was no one to help me yet somehow I had to get him to have more confidence in himself. We had gone down this path so many times, the ups and the downs. I wasn't about to give up; I had to somehow find the answer to yet another nightmare.

I knew the person he was when he wasn't out of control. He was the kindest-hearted human being anyone could ever meet. He had always been so health conscious and could have done anything he set his mind to. When anyone takes any type of substance—be it alcohol or anything else—it changes them completely. They don't realise what is happening to them or what they put anyone else through.

Why I have to go down this path over and over is unreal to me. I had been through enough in my life and was going through so many emotions but I couldn't let it get the better of me.

He promised me that he would stop behaving this way and start concentrating on making his life better. His building class had been cancelled for two weeks and a friend had got him a trial with his boss to become an apprentice plumber for a few days. I felt he was grasping at straws but it would keep him focused for a few days.

Then maybe then he would realise what he really wanted.

My son's best friend, Dave, was always there for both the boys when they needed someone to lean on. He had known them since primary school and had been through his own problems because of divorce but had managed to carve out his career earlier than most. Both the boys respected him for what he had achieved. He was like a brother to them.

It seems there are many young people in this generation who think life owes them something, that it is just one big party. They are not like the generations before us when we had to take on responsibility at such a young age. When I think about Bryce, even though he was on his own from 17 years of age, he certainly didn't turn out to be any different. He took no responsibility at all for anyone but himself. I suppose I sound angry and I am!

Sometimes, I think my life could have been so different had it not been for Bryce. Maybe I would have been much happier had I not met him but then I would not have my sons. That is a blessing in itself for many reasons. Maybe that is what it was all about.

Even though my life has been far from normal, I am grateful I have the boys in my life, warts and all. At least they know the meaning of family.

I had sold another two properties and I was excited because I was nearly at the point where I had paid my retainer back and could start seeing some commission.

John was going away for a week, which gave me an opportunity to make some in-roads whilst he was gone. I wanted to list and sell more than I had before. I was the best at what I did and was starting to believe it. Much to my surprise, work was becoming my saviour. It was my turn and I was about to embark on a new journey. One that would see me financially independent, which was what I had always hoped for.

In these past six years—actually nearly seven now—I have learned so much. It has been the hardest road travelled but the knowledge I have now will give me the success for which I have yearned.

It's all about hard work, patience and discipline. Those three cornerstones can take you to wherever you want to be in life. I had learned that looking back creates so much negativity and that alone had stopped me from moving forward but I was in a good space now. Just had to keep focused on my goal. When I talk about financial independence, it is not all about money. It was about success and regaining my self-esteem that had been stripped away from me since I was 17 years of age.

My eldest sister had called me and invited me away with her family. It wasn't for another month and I needed the money so I could get away. It would only be for a few days but it was important to me to have some time to relax and it had been so many years since we had all spent quality time together.

Chapter 22

EMPOWERING MYSELF

I had finished my boring Sunday reading *The Law of Attraction*. It was always good to fill my head with positive thoughts before I went to sleep. I had read this book some years prior and thought it was time to reinforce what I already knew.

The next morning I arrived at work earlier than usual. John was away and had entrusted the office to me for the week. It didn't start off too well as one of our vendors had decided not to accept one of my contracts for the purchase of his property but my attitude was to stay positive and believe someone else would come along.

However, I did list a property in the afternoon. John and I had presented to the vendor together to get the listing, and I had been left to do the work. So, I was at least hoping he would share the commission with me.

I had decided that this was the week that was going to see me with a sale. That is what I would focus on. Nothing was going to interfere with my thoughts. I even started meditating every morning, giving me a clear head before I started work. I had never mastered meditation. Not sure why. More likely it was just that I couldn't turn off my thoughts and the many self-help books I had read all said meditation was a great way to start and finish the day.

Everything takes time but it is always hard when you are waiting for your life to change. It was patience I was lacking; I found it hard to wait for anything. All the success that one is supposed to experience in life takes so long to happen.

Was it just me who felt like that? Or is everyone the same? After all, I had done everything *The Secret* had told me.

I had read the book and watched the video twice but still couldn't see myself making inroads. It was then I realised maybe that was the problem. I had to retrain the way I thought to start to see positive outcomes. To see and feel the end result of where I wanted to be. It's all about thoughts matching your feelings – they must be the same. You have to feel as if it has already happened.

That excitement, that feeling of such confidence makes all the difference in the world. Just imagine if you had no doubts in yourself and you just sailed through life, it would be like winning Tatts Lotto. I think what I am trying to say is having faith in yourself is the beginning of success.

I was starting to tune in to my positive side and knew it was only a matter of time before I would feel that type of power. It was all about time and continual persistence. I always kept top of my mind the *Law of Attraction* and what it would bring.

As I said, the vendor did not accept the contract but that same morning a man appeared in the office who I had not seen before. He asked me about some properties I had on the waterfront and I gave him the one I hadn't sold because of the vendor not accepting the former offer. I stayed positive and that same afternoon a woman, who was the gentleman's wife who had come in earlier, appeared in the office. She asked me to show her through the property. They were not interested in the home only the land as they were looking to build their dream home. As soon as she saw it, she put in an offer $100,000 more than the previous I had presented to the vendor.

I was over the moon and thinking the law of attraction does work; however, I had to wait another three days to see whether the sale would go through. So, I decided I would use the law of attraction every time I thought of my two boys. Particularly the eldest.

He appeared to be extremely stressed starting his building course and he had become very hard to live with. I needed to stop and think differently towards him. Needed to stop focusing on his behaviour and start to see him in a different light.

No matter what happened and what mood he was in, I kept my focus on his career, seeing him as a great builder. This was going to take time but in my mind I knew one day my thoughts would become reality. I kept telling him how well he was doing and in turn, I knew that he would start believing in himself.

As parents, maybe we lose sight of the bigger picture and that actually is what is missing in every aspect of our lives. We don't believe in ourselves enough or those around us. It's funny when you start to change the way you think. Everything starts to change around you and you start to see things as they should be.

The offer on the property I was hoping for didn't go through but I was not about to give up. I had come too far and knew I had to stay focused. What I needed was to concentrate on my negotiating skills to get this deal through.

At first, the purchasers at first were hesitant to make another offer but I just stayed focused, knowing in the end I would win. Every night for a week I would wake up in the morning and go to bed at night visualising the sold sign on the property. It was going to happen! The purchasers raised their price twice but still the vendor wanted more. By this time, I was becoming frustrated. The property I felt was not worth more than what had been offered. We were up to $1,145,000, and it still wasn't enough.

It was coming down to the wire; the vendor had changed his mind and dropped the price to $1,175,000. Was this ever going to end? Negotiations had gone on for a week; I wanted this sale to come to fruition and although it was exhausting, it was also a great learning curve for me.

Remember I said I was always impatient? I could never wait for anything personally or professionally, which was my problem. This experience was what I needed to be successful.

I had always been of the belief that everything happens for a reason, and that had become so clear after this experience.

Whilst I was waiting for this deal to come to an end, I picked up another two listings. Everything was moving forward, and I was ridiculously excited!

It was all going to happen for me. The life I finally deserved.

Every now and again I would fantasise about the perfect man I would like in my life but, as I said to my dear friend Kristee, whom I worked with, I had come to the stage in my life if I couldn't have the best then I would rather have nothing. Financial independence had become so important to me after so many losses. I knew that the universe was teaching me the patience and discipline I needed to make my dreams come true.

My daughter finally had come back in my life, although after looking at her Facebook site, I felt a sense of betrayal. She had gone away on holidays with her father, stepmother, close friends and my eldest son's family. They were having a wonderful holiday and didn't care at all about me or what their younger brothers were going through. We weren't welcome at all; none of them wanted us there. I wanted my family so badly to be a family but I could not compromise my principles. My eldest son and daughter, even though they were my children, did not take after me. They were more their father's children, and frankly, they had proven to me that I was not that important to them anymore.

Whether there are two children in a family or six, every child is born with their own personality. While they are brought up in the same family, their principles and values can be all so different.

By this time, I was completely over it and my daughter was so oblivious to what was right and wrong where family was concerned. She did not understand what loyalty meant; or maybe she did, but her loyalty was not to me. I could not understand how she could put her sister-in law before me. This woman was married to my eldest son; and had caused so many problems in my family since I had bought the restaurant. She had no conscience at all.

I knew at this point I couldn't try and salvage anything. My family was never going to be perfect or anywhere close to it. My daughter and her brother were people I really didn't know. I loved all my children unconditionally, I just didn't understand why they were so hurtful. Family was everything to me and I had tried to give all my children everything they needed but I had come to realise that there was obviously something that maybe I didn't get right.

My younger boys had always been so different, and as inconsiderate as they could be sometimes, they still had compassion for others. I knew they were no different to me as far as their principles and values were concerned.

I decided I was not going to allow my thoughts to stray. That I had to keep focused on my life and reject all the negative thoughts I would have from time to time to stay on track if I was going to make it on my own.

By this time, I believed so much in the *Law of Attraction* and I was so focused on my future. I could not force my eldest children to be closer to me and I had made up my mind just to accept the way they felt about me and move on with my life.

The only thing that I needed to focus on was closing my deal and getting on with it. Nothing else was important to me at that time.

I was a tough negotiator and I knew this deal was going to happen. Life had been exhausting and lonely to say the least since Bryce and I divorced but I have to say, I have learned so many valuable lessons for which I am grateful. Even though I am still by myself, my experiences in life have taught me that whatever life throws at me, I know I will cope.

The eldest of my younger boys was really getting his life together, and I was so proud. He had given up all his addictions and was completely focused on his building career. Life was changing again and I was starting to see my younger boys getting their lives on track. That is all I ever wanted. For them to realise they could be whoever they wanted to be. Out of all my children, clearly they were the ones who had the principles of life that were so important to me. I was grateful for that because they had gone through so much over the past six years. They deserved to be happy.

My eldest of the two had met a lovely young woman named Beth, who I am hoping will be by his side for a long time. I believe she was his inspiration. Isn't that how the old saying goes? Behind every successful man, there is always a good woman.

The coming week was going to be interesting as I hoped to sell at least three properties and list a couple more. I was starting to see glimpses of what I could achieve. Life was starting to be wonderful again and I knew if I continued to monitor my thoughts and feelings, I would make it all happen. I truly believe that is the secret to success.

As *The Law of Attraction* tells us, every time you have a negative thought change it to a positive and everything will be as it should be. It truly does work and I think that is what makes the difference between success and failure. Just imagine if there were no bad thoughts, we would all be very successful and life would be a much happier place. I only wish it had not taken me all these years to understand the importance of monitoring thoughts and how easy it is to change the way we think and feel.

Visualisation also plays an important part of making dreams a reality. I wanted so badly to sell a property close to my heart for the vendors, so I wrote sold across the flyer I had on my desk and imagined it sold. A few days later it did sell, it was truly amazing.

My big sale finally went through and then for the next month I listed another 12 homes and sold eight. My goal was to be the best and that was exactly where I was heading, I had no doubt.

Looking back, I could see where I had been. The emotions I had experienced through bad relationships. The decisions I had made whilst going through emotional turmoil, ending in disaster. Finally, for the first time, I was starting to experience my own life and that was what all the lessons were about... as painful as they were.

I am confident now in whom I am, and I now know the world is my oyster. I hope that one day I will find the relationship I so richly deserve and have waited all my life for but I am in no hurry.

Life can be great and none of what I went through was really necessary. Had I listened to my instincts and learned to control my emotions, things would have been different. That is the key to keeping your sanity. I have learned so much about the pattern of our thoughts and how powerful our mind really is. I have let go of my anger, rejection, hate, fear and feelings of betrayal.

We can be whoever we want to be no matter our

background. I have come to love my life now and I know I will have continued success no matter what lies ahead.

I now know discipline and patience.

I have four wonderful children and I am proud of them all no matter what has happened between us. My eldest son, Jack, even though he has hurt me so deeply has no idea of what I think of him, which I find sad. I am and have always been proud of him. He does a very difficult job as a psychiatric nurse and I do admire him for that every day of my life.

My successful daughter, Summer, who is so special to me, I will cherish forever. She is not only beautiful but has her own successful business and an amazing life. I know she will always find her way.

My two youngest sons are finally on their way to successful lives. I waited so long but I know now it will happen. Even though they had an absentee father, they have learned so many valuable lessons. When or if they have children, they will understand more than most the value of being a great dad and I know for sure they will be the best dad a child could have.

My youngest son, Luke, is on his way to becoming a teacher and my eldest son, Craig, a great builder.

I am so proud of their achievements and grateful for everyday they are part of my life.

They truly know and understand the true meaning of family.

I will leave you with something always to remember.

Life was never meant to be easy, and all families face controversy with each other but please always remember, have your say and get over it because nothing is worth losing family.

Success is not just about your work, it is also about family.

I call it unconditional love.

Family is a circle of strength and love

THE END

ABOUT THE AUTHOR

Suzanna James was born in Queensland. Her parents moved to a small town in Victoria in the late fifties and Suzanna was the middle child of three girls. She did not have an easy family life which is one of the reasons that family became so important to her. She has always dreamed of having the perfect family she never had (apart from her loving mother), but that was never to be.

www.ingramcontent.com/pod-product-compliance
Lightning Source LLC
Chambersburg PA
CBHW031246290426
44109CB00012B/463